Raising
Happy Hearts

Dana Bellamy

ISBN: 978-0-692-08655-1

Dedication

I dedicate this book to my loving husband, William Bellamy Jr., and our six children: Kiera, Jerome, Grace, Lily, Judah, and Justin.

Will, I wouldn't be the wife and mother I am today if it weren't for your sacrificial, Christlike love toward me and our family. Through your leadership, you have provided an environment where our children and I have flourished. You are my best friend, and I thank God for you!

Kiera, Jerome, Grace, Lily, Judah, and Justin, I am so proud of each of you. You are my treasures, gifted to me from our heavenly Father. You bring me such joy every day. I am thankful to be your mother. I am looking forward to watching you grow in your relationship with the Lord and to seeing you live blessed and prosperous lives to His glory.

Acknowledgments

First, I want to give the biggest thank-you to my heavenly Father, my Lord and Savior, Jesus Christ, and my precious Holy Spirit for everything You are to me. Words cannot express how much I love You!

I would also like to give a special thank-you to my husband, Will, for being a constant support and encouragement to me throughout our marriage. This book wouldn't have come to fruition without you.

I would also like to extend a warm thank-you to Yeamah Logan for all her help with this book. Your guidance was key to helping me get started.

Special thanks goes to Russell Whipkey and Emily Heath for blessing me with the photos for this book, and to Kristen Price for designing the book cover so beautifully.

A huge thank-you also goes to Saleena Bellamy, John Greer, Shoshana Buckendorf and Stephanie Johnson for sacrificially sowing into the creation of this book. You are true godsends!

I also want to recognize and thank Rich Kanyali, Jessica Heinz, Nicole Dominy, Geri Gardner, Mary Lacy, Bryan Houser, Carol Price, and Katelyn Bellard for their valuable input and time spent helping me, and Sylvia Wells for her attention to detail and help in proofreading this book.

I couldn't have done this without you all. Thank you!

Dana Bellamy

Foreword

When I was growing up, I was not the motherly type with loads of dolls that all had names and wardrobes. Instead, I was imagining jungle safari mission trips, or Egyptian camel outreaches to desert tribes. Now, this wasn't saying I didn't like children. As the oldest of six I was practically on mommy duty with my mom from eight years old. I would babysit other's kids and was good at it. Yet I also knew I was going to be going around the world ministering.

My younger sister, on the other hand, had a mercy gift that just yelled, "I'm going to be a mom of a ton of kids!" She was always giving me a hard time when I talked about raising kids, as she said that the only reason I wanted to have kids was to raise more ministers.

Well the way I saw it then, and still now, is that *yes* God has given us precious lives for His glory and the purposes He has on our children's lives! We get the privilege of shaping lovers of God on a daily basis! Yet with the everyday work load, pressures, expectations, failures, and frustrations of parenthood, there are questions that come up. Are we doing a good job? Why does it seem so hard sometimes? How do we make sure our children become the amazing individuals God created them to be? Where do we find wisdom for those really tough moments?

Raising Happy Hearts is a book of bright encouragement, and a realignment of what's important for what God has called you to do. As you read, you'll be inspired to be the parent God has enabled you to be, with no comparison to anyone else around you. You will see in a powerful way that raising children is one of "high calling," no less in God's eyes than other roles. In fact, raising, serving, and loving your children is doing everything unto Jesus himself.

This book is a gold-mine of powerful truths for the new mom and dad treading in the new waters of raising babies! Yet this book isn't just for the new parents blessed with their young ones, but also for those that are already in the race of parenthood. Dana's writing is filled with life-giving practical training for those moments that the enemy tries to lie about your life, marriage, children, and future. Training that isn't just words, but as you will see as you read, that they are proven principles that work!

As you read this, may you be as encouraged as I was again. That you have a beautiful, powerful call of God on your life to raise, love, and fashion the lives He's entrusted to you. That you do not have to be overwhelmed or confused because you have the Holy Spirit alongside of you to lead you and guide you into all understanding! Having a peaceful marriage, and joyful children are the very desires of God's heart for you.

As you go through these powerful chapters, let the

Lord show you practical and powerful truths for your family. Truths, that as you apply, will show forth such beautiful and joyful lives in a world needing to see that you can truly - Raise Happy Hearts!!

Carrie Pickett

Honored mother of two beautiful children: Elliana Grace and Michael Patrick. Director of World Outreach Training Operations for Andrew Wommack Ministries and Charis Bible College, and co-founder of Equip Ministries International.

Endorsement

Raising Happy Hearts is one of the best books on raising secure, loved, and happy children I have read. It covers the essential principles of raising emotionally healthy children with a great balance between love and discipline. Will and Dana Bellamy are good friends of mine who are great parents and have modeled the principles Dana teaches in this book. I highly recommend this book to parents, soon to be parents, and grandparents. You will be equipped and blessed by reading Raising Happy Hearts.

Greg Mohr
Director of Charis Bible College
Woodland Park, Colorado

Contents

Preface

In the Word of God, Titus 2:3-4 states:

Likewise, teach the older women to be reverent in the way they live, not to be slanderers or addicted to much wine, but to teach what is good. Then they can urge the younger women to love their husbands and children, to be self-controlled and pure, to be busy at home, to be kind, and to be subject to their husbands, so that no one will malign the word of God.

New International Version

Over the years that I have been a mother, the Lord has tenderly taken my hand and taught me many things about raising my own happy kids.

I am not an expert by any means, and I have definitely not "arrived." However, I believe the Lord has shown me that the principles and revelations He has given me in the area of being a wife, mother, and His child will be a blessing and a help to many other wives and mothers throughout the world.

The voice of the world shouts very loudly. It tells us what is "normal." The problem is, the world's idea of normal is generally the complete opposite of God's way of doing things and the way His kingdom operates. I believe this book will shed more light on what God intended for families and will help silence the voice of the world.

My hope is that through this book, many women will be empowered to raise their own happy hearts!

Introduction

When I first became a mother, I felt completely unprepared and inadequate. When I was heavily pregnant with my first child, I had feelings of fear and worry because I knew that I had no experience with what to do to take care of a baby. I made a comment to my own mother, "I am worried that I will not know what to do, because I have never had a baby before." My mother, who is a mother of five herself, tried to comfort me by replying, "Don't worry. She's never had a mom before." This brought a smile to my face, but it was of little comfort.

When my daughter was born, I learned little by little how to take care of and nurture the little life entrusted to me. I remember it being a huge adjustment, and on many occasions, it felt overwhelming. Many times I felt like a failure, and at times I experienced depression and anxiety. A woman at my church prophesied to me when I was newly pregnant. She said, among other things, "You will be a great wife and mother." I believed it wholeheartedly at the time, yet after my baby was born and I was in the throes of motherhood with a newborn, I cried out, "She lied!"

It has been many years since then, and I have six children now. The Lord has shown me so much about raising kids as I have yielded to Him and allowed Him to coach me through it. After all, who knows better how to raise children than the One who created them and loves them more than life itself, which He proved by His sacrifice on the cross?

God has shown me not only how to best care for my children's physical needs, but also how to best nurture their emotional and spiritual needs. I hope this book will be a blessing to you and your children.

I. The Importance of Motherhood to God

When I had only two children, I started serving in my local church. I could only do a certain amount of serving because my children were young and needed a lot of my time and attention. One day I was pondering this while my two children were playing in the bath. I thought about how much I was hindered in doing "the work of the Lord" because of my children. I reasoned that it would be wisdom to limit my family to only these two children because as they grew up, I would have more time to devote to my "holy service to God" and not have to use most of my time raising kids. I know this sounds terrible, but I believed at the time that my train of thought was noble and even pleasing to God—until I heard God's unmistakable voice speak to me very clearly, "Where are the three children I have called you to raise?"

This stopped me in my tracks. I knew without a shadow of a doubt that the Lord was telling me that He didn't want me to stop at the two children that I had, and that my children *were* my ministry!

Mr. Normal and Mr. Talented

You see, the Lord had just echoed a statement that came from a well-known Bible teacher I had traveled to see while he was teaching live one night. He was talking about the time in eternity when believers will stand before the judgment seat of God as He hands out the heavenly rewards for work done on earth. (This is not the judgment where the Lord separates the believers from the unbelievers. Salvation is not judged by works and is not received by works. It is received by faith. Only one question will be asked there: "Did you believe in My Son Jesus and trust Him alone for your salvation?" If the answer is yes, you're in!)

In the Bible teacher's story, God was giving out rewards, but believers were not judged by what we did. We were judged in the light of what God had called us to do. The teacher quoted Ecclesiastes 3:15, which reads, *"That which is has already been, and what is to be has already been; And God requires an account of what is past."*

God has every single day of our lives written in His book. He already knows what He has destined for each and every one of us to do. If we ask Him, He will show us what His perfect will is and will give us the grace to walk in it. Or we can choose our own path outside of His will.

If we do exactly what God has destined us to do, we will get the full measure of our reward in heaven. God is just. Each and every one of us will get the full reward for doing what we were gifted to do, regardless of whether it is a fivefold ministry position, a position in the home, or a marketplace position. It can also be both a marketplace position and a position in the home, depending on the season of our lives that we are in. Once our children are grown, God's will for us doesn't stagnate. He has planned every season in our lives perfectly, and none of us are forgotten. We are also never too old to fulfill our calling. There is no such thing as retirement in the kingdom of God.

God makes this truth very clear in the parable of the talents. Just as an example, let's say that God gave one man a measure of ten talents. We will call this man Mr. Talented. Mr. Talented lived his life and only used eight of his ten talents. He did a lot, but he ultimately fell short of all the Lord had given him the grace to do. He will receive his heavenly reward based on how he performed in relation to the talents he received, not based on what he did in comparison to the people around him. Now, let's say that God gave another man two talents. We will call this man Mr. Normal. Mr. Normal trusted God and obeyed Him and used all two talents for the glory of God.

From a natural perspective, we would not know that Mr. Talented was given ten talents. We also would not know that he was only using eight of them. Yet we would judge him and think, *Wow! He is so talented. Look at how much he is doing for the kingdom! Look at all the people he is reaching for the Lord.* Then we would look at Mr. Normal. We also would not know that he was given only two talents and was being a good and faithful steward of those two talents. Yet we would judge him and think, *That guy is insignificant. He can't hold a candle to Mr. Talented. He is not producing nearly as much fruit and will definitely not get as great a reward in heaven as Mr. Talented will.*

From a heavenly perspective, however, Mr. Normal will receive a greater reward at the judgment seat of God than Mr. Talented because he was a faithful steward of all the Lord gave him, even though his two talents were not very highly esteemed by the world. Conversely, Mr. Talented was only a faithful steward of 80 percent of the talents entrusted to him. He will only receive 80 percent of his heavenly reward.

During his day-to-day life, Mr. Talented could have possibly compared himself with Mr. Normal and decided that he was accomplishing much more than Mr. Normal would ever be able to. He then could have simply rested on his achievements without focusing on God and all that God had called him to do. This would have been a big mistake. That is why it says in 2 Corinthians 10:12, *"For we dare not class ourselves or compare ourselves with those who commend themselves. But they, measuring themselves by themselves, and comparing themselves among themselves, are not wise."*

The Trap of Comparison

As we can see, according to Scripture, it is foolish to compare ourselves with others and what they are or are not doing. Yet how many times do we compare ourselves with other women and mothers and decide that we are not measuring up? I know I am guilty of this. Yet we do not know what God has equipped others to do or how many talents God has entrusted them with. We also don't know how many of those talents they are using! Only God knows. So, stop comparing yourself with your neighbor. Look solely to God and do what He has told you to do, regardless of what it looks like to the world. After all, are we looking for the praises of men or the praises of God? No one will be standing with us at the throne of God (except for Jesus). We are ultimately responsible for what we do or do not do in this world. God gave us our will, and He will not violate it. We need to choose to live our lives in obedience to Him and for His glory!

What God has asked you to do may not look very significant to the world, but we cannot judge heavenly things by worldly standards. Everything we do affects the people around us. If we just do what God called us to do, we will affect people for the kingdom of God for eternity. Our lives are all linked, and we are all working together as a body, the body of Christ. The world needs accountants, restauranteurs, entertainers, bakers, fishermen, bankers, mothers, and fathers. If we were all pastors, teachers, evangelists, and apostles, who would deliver our mail and take away our trash? Who would grow our food and fly us around the world? And who would raise the children?

Children Are Ministry

This brings me to my point. As I was listening to this well-known teacher, he asked, "Where are the three children I have called you to raise?" My friend was sitting next to me. She leaned over toward me and whispered, "That was meant for you." I did not need her to tell me that. Those words had already penetrated right into my core. I knew that God was speaking to me. This is what He brought to my remembrance as I was giving my children their bath. My children *are* my ministry. I did not need to look elsewhere, outside the home. I was already at the center of His will.

I knew that if I put my focus on raising my children, I would be a good and faithful steward of all the talents that the Lord had entrusted to me in this season of life. Every life that He blesses me with is of great importance to Him. Molding and shaping little innocent lives is a high calling!

The world would have you believe that being a full-time mother is insignificant. Full-time mothers are often looked down upon compared with career women, women who are pursuing their dreams and traveling the world, or even women in the ministry! Yet Jesus said in Luke 9:48, *"Whoever receives this little child in My name receives Me; and whoever receives Me receives Him who sent Me. For he who is least among you all will be great."* How profound! As full-time mothers, we are seen to be the least on earth. Yet we receive little children from the hand of the Father and, in doing so, receive Jesus and the heavenly Father Himself. This scripture shows, once and for all, that mothers are great in the kingdom of heaven.

Many faithful mothers who have poured into their children will be thoroughly surprised when they get to heaven and find that they are honored among the greats! Yet that is the truth. What greater calling is there than raising up children who know and love the Lord? However, if I were to neglect my children to pursue a ministry outside the home, not only would that not be pleasing to God, but it would also be detrimental to His calling on my life: my children. Knowing this, I try to make God, my husband, and our children my priority and focus in my day-to-day life.

A High Calling

Let's think for a minute. Would you say that Mary, the mother of Jesus, had a high calling? If she did nothing else with her life than raise Jesus faithfully and to the best of her ability, wouldn't it be obvious that she fulfilled her destiny and would be greatly honored in heaven?

How about Elizabeth, the mother of John the Baptist? We would think the same thing.

Luke 7:28 states:

For I say to you, among those born of women there is not a greater prophet than John the Baptist; but he who is least in the kingdom of God is greater than he.

And 1 Corinthians 12:27 states, *"Now you are the body of Christ, and each one of you is a part of it"(NIV).*

These two scriptures make it very clear that raising our children with faithfulness and excellence is a high calling, just like it was for the mother of Jesus and the mother of John the Baptist. These mothers show us that every child we raise is greater in the kingdom of God than John the Baptist and is an integral part of the body of Christ, which is the body of Jesus Himself, who is the Head of the church.

So, our calling is in no way inferior to Mary's and Elizabeth's. We are raising up generations who will do greater works than Jesus did. He Himself said so. We know He is truth, and only truth proceeds from His mouth. That prophecy will be fulfilled. And who will fulfill it if we don't have faithful mothers who will raise their children up in the love of the Lord and teach them His Word?

Therefore, since we can see that being faithful, godly mothers and raising our children well is a high calling bestowed upon us by God Himself, let us do it wholeheartedly, with focus and determination and with a spirit of excellence. If we were called to pastor a church of 2,000, we would make sure that we gave it all we had. After all, we would have 2,000 souls entrusted to our care. So, let us mother our children with the view that, in God's eyes, it is not less important that we have been entrusted with a few souls.

A few souls are not less important than many souls. We know that in the Scripture, it says that Jesus left the ninety-nine sheep to search for one that was lost. Every soul is precious to the Father. Every one.

God entrusted you with the children you have (and with those you will have). So, be a good steward over these precious gifts from the Father.

Charitable Deeds

Matthew 6:1-4 states:

> *Take heed that you do not do your charitable deeds before men, to be seen by them. Otherwise you have no reward from your Father in heaven. Therefore, when you do a* **charitable deed***, do not sound a trumpet before you as the hypocrites do in the synagogues and in the streets, that they may have glory from men. Assuredly, I say to you, they have their reward. But when you do a charitable deed, do not let your left hand know what your right hand is doing, that your charitable deed may be in secret; and your Father who sees in secret will Himself reward you openly.*

On www.oxforddictionaries.com, the word *charitable* is defined as "1. Relating to the assistance of those in need. 1.2. Generous in giving to those in need. 2. Apt to judge others leniently or favourably." According to this same website, the origin of the word *charitable* is

"Middle English (in the sense 'showing Christian love to God and man')."

The charitable deeds that the Lord was talking about here are not merely limited to those we do outside the home. Who is more needy and more dependent upon us than our own children? Every act of service performed in the home through love will produce a heavenly reward. No wonder mothers will be so honored in heaven. We put others' needs in front of our own all day long and are storing up abundant heavenly treasure in storehouses. That's good news!

So, faithful mother, you are extremely important to God. I know that when you're at home raising your kids, life can seem repetitive and monotonous. But we need to realize that every time we faithfully serve our husband and children, God sees, and we are storing up treasures in heaven. Think about that when you're cleaning the kitchen or folding the laundry for the umpteenth time. All of your service is creating a stable and blessed home life for your husband and children, and God sees every little thing that you do in service to others.

Dana Bellamy

II. Loved Children Are Happy Children

It is no secret that loved children are happy children. God put a need in each one of us to feel loved. It is one of our greatest needs.

The Five Love Languages

I have read *The Five Love Languages* by Gary Chapman and *The Five Love Languages of Children* by Gary Chapman and Ross Campbell. In his books, Chapman explains that there are five distinct "languages" (or ways) in which we each give and receive love. The five languages are words of affirmation, physical touch, quality time, acts of service, and gifts. (If you haven't done so already, it will be very beneficial for you to read one or both of these books on your own.)

It is important for me to touch on the content of the latter book, because if your children don't feel loved by you, your training/instruction will not be effective and they will also not be happy children. As you can see, this is an integral part of raising happy kids.

A lot of the time we *show* love in the primary love language that we understand and love to receive. Unfortunately, if we have a child who doesn't have the same primary love language as we do, they will not understand that we are showing our love to them. For instance, if we have a child whose primary love language is physical touch, and ours is words of affirmation, we can tell them all day long how much we love them and how wonderful we think they are. Yet if we don't also show our love through hugs, kisses, play-wrestling, etc., our child will think, *Why doesn't my mom touch me? If she loved me, she would touch me.* Or your child could think, *I know my mom loves me, but she doesn't show it.*

The same things goes for all of the other love languages. You can watch your children to find clues as to what their love languages are, and also ask the Holy Spirit to highlight to you the primary love languages of each of your children. Once He does, you need to make sure that you speak that language to them, as well as sprinkling in the other four languages on occasion. That way, your children will know that you love them and will be secure in that love.

Discovering Your Child's Love Language

When the Lord began highlighting this truth to me, I started to feel a little overwhelmed. After all, I have six children, and it's possible that they could all have completely different love languages! I didn't want to fail any of them. The Lord quickly spoke to my heart, "Don't worry.

I have given you the grace you need to love your kids the way they need to be loved." That gave me a lot of comfort. My husband and I then tried to figure out the love languages of each of our children.

Our oldest two were easy. We just asked them what made them feel loved. They both responded that family time made them feel loved. Their primary love language is obviously quality time. Then we have two other children who are constantly coming up to us for affection (hugs and kisses, etc.). Their primary love language is physical touch. Another child likes to frequently give us words of affirmation. She will say, "Mama, I love you," or "Mama, you have beautiful hair." So, I believe that her primary love language must be words of affirmation. The sixth is still a baby, so we will continue to shower him in all five languages until he is old enough to show us which one makes him feel more loved. I have already ascertained that his primary love language is not 'physical touch,' as he already tries to escape my hugs and kisses, unfortunately!

Mommy's and Daddy's Love Language

It is also important to know your own primary love language and that of your spouse. If you are not speaking your spouse's primary love language to them, they will feel unloved or unappreciated by you, no matter how much you try to show them (in your own love language).

For me, physical touch doesn't come as easily as words of affirmation (which is my primary love language). Yet physical touch is the primary love language of my husband and two of my children. So, I have to get out of my comfort zone and show affection regardless. It would be a tragedy if my husband or any of my children felt that I didn't love them because I only expressed it to them in words of affirmation.

Love Tank

Everybody has a "love tank." When people we love express love to us in our own love language, our tanks get filled up. It is important that we show love to our husband and kids in their primary love languages so that they are not trying to do life with empty tanks. This would not be beneficial for them at all.

For instance, when husbands have empty tanks, they cannot function at optimal levels when they are at work or out in public. Let's say that your husband's primary love language is words of affirmation, but you only show him love by serving him in different ways (since your primary love language is acts of service). Even though you are doing a great job (in your mind) of showering him with love, He will feel like you don't appreciate him since you don't ever tell him so. Your husband's love tank will be running on empty day after day as he goes to work.

If there is a woman at work who has ulterior motives and constantly gives him compliments such as "You look great today!" or "Great job!" he may feel that he is appreciated more at work than at home, even though that is not the case. Not only that, he may have to fight the urge to desire the attention of the other woman. I am not saying that he would be unfaithful, but he would definitely not be as happy as he would be with a full love tank. He would definitely prefer to get that affirmation from you, his wife. We want to give our husbands what they need to withstand all the wiles of the Enemy.

If your husband goes to work with his love tank full, knowing that he is loved by his wife, he will be able to perform at optimal levels in his work and will not be craving attention from others.

Your Children's Love Tanks

As for your children, when their love tanks are full and they know that they are unconditionally loved, they will not seek love in all the wrong places as they get older. Not only that, they will be much easier to train and will have a firm foundation on which to flourish in life. Sometimes kids act out at home and at school. Many times this is just a cry for attention. When we show our kids, in their primary love language, that we love them, we fulfill that need for attention. Thus, they won't have a need to act out anymore. They will have full love tanks and will be secure in our love for them.

When my third child was three years old, my husband and I tried diligently to train her to be obedient like her older two siblings. It seemed like no matter how consistent we were in training her, she continued her disobedient behavior. I was really frustrated with the situation and with my daughter. I couldn't understand why I was able to easily train my oldest two children, but my third was proving to be a curve ball.

Every time I asked the Lord what I should do with her, He only ever replied, "Love her." I didn't understand what He was trying to say to me. I did love her, so how could that be the answer? Not long after, the Lord brought to our attention that her primary love language is physical touch.

Although we were affectionate with her, we needed to increase it, since her love tank wasn't full. My husband and I started to pay better attention to the amount of affection we gave her to make sure that we filled her love tank. My husband even took her to the store, just the two of them, and lavished her with affection. He let her ride the kiddie ride at the store, and they even ate donuts together. We were delighted to witness a turnaround in her behavior. She began to settle down and become just as content, loving, and obedient as her older siblings.

Even before I knew about love languages, the love tanks of my older two children were full all the time since I was a homeschooling mother and fulfilled their need for quality time effortlessly. But now I see why there was such a difference between them and my third child.

Daddy-Daughter Dates

Another thing I have learned is that it is important for daddies to take their daughters on one-on-one outings. I liked to call these daddy-daughter dates. This is quality, uninterrupted time when a daughter receives love from her father. It also teaches her, through her father's example, how a man is meant to treat a woman. When she is grown, she will have her father as a standard and won't settle for a man who doesn't treat her as precious, like her father does.

Daddies also need that one-on-one time with their sons. Sons will learn valuable skills from their fathers, such as mechanical skills, fishing skills, and survival skills. This will show them that they are loved by their dads, and they will also learn life skills that they can draw on and cultivate in adulthood.

Make a goal together for your husband to spend one-on-one quality time with each of his children one time per month. During this time, he should withhold any and all instruction or correction. This is a time for only connection and fellowship. This is to be an enjoyably fun time for the children to share with their dad. Another thing to note is that it doesn't even have to involve money. Just doing simple things like going for a nature walk together will have the desired effect, as long as your child enjoys doing that.

Dana Bellamy

III. Guarding the Hearts of Your Children

God looks at our heart motives and not just our actions. God does not care as much about *what* we do as *why* we do it. Therefore, we will give God a great gift if we are diligent to steward the hearts of our children so that their actions are godly and stem from a desire to be pleasing to the Lord and a true blessing to people.

I always thought that raising kids would get easier as they got older, but that is not true. Yes, they are easier to take care of physically, but stewarding their hearts can be a lot more complex and challenging.

Thankfully, God helps me watch over the hearts of my children every day. He is always helping me to be aware of any negative attitudes or any deeper issues that are arising in their hearts. He also gives me the wisdom that I need to help my children get out of any traps of the Enemy and get back into a place of victory.

For instance, my oldest used to deal with unforgiveness and anger toward her much younger sisters. Her younger sisters were just being little kids, but they often would not listen to her, and it frustrated her a lot. She also claimed that they would report to me that she was doing things that she really wasn't, and that I would correct her unjustly. This caused her to be offended at them and to feel anger toward them.

The Lord brought the situation to my attention and gave us some alone time for her to really share with me what was on her heart. The Lord gave me wisdom in this situation as I asked Him for help, and we were able to resolve it. I was able to pray over her and impart wisdom to her about the situation. She got a breakthrough at that time, and now she is able to respond to her sisters with a lot more peace. She no longer deals with unforgiveness and anger toward them.

Our children, just like us, will deal with things throughout their lives. I have found that when I partner with the Holy Spirit and the grace that is available to me, He leads me and guides me and helps me to nip every negative situation in the bud and guide my children into living victorious lives. He loves my kids more than I do, and He truly is my ever present help in time of need. There has never been a problem for which the Lord hasn't provided a wonderful solution. He is such a great Father!

As believers, we are not parenting in the dark. It is not a blind-leading-the-blind scenario. God has opened our eyes so that we can see clearly. Unbelievers parent the way that they think is right to their understanding. Unfortunately, their understanding is often not based on truth and will lead to a whole host of issues for their children. But as believers, we don't need to guess. We have the Word of God and the direction of the Holy Spirit to light our path so that we can see clearly the direction to take to reach the desired outcome. I read a Facebook post a couple of years back, posted by an acquaintance. She asked this question: "Does anybody else worry that they are ruining their kids?" We don't need to have that worry. As we seek the Lord and follow the leading of the Holy Spirit, He will show us practically what to do with our children so that they will be healthy and whole and on the way to fulfilling their awesome destiny in Him. He will show us when our children are dealing with issues that need to be corrected.

It is not difficult to steward the hearts of our children. Ask for and receive God's grace in this area. We are not parenting alone. God never planned for us to try to parent our children without Him. That is just a recipe for disaster. We need to be mindful that God is always with us at every moment of our lives. He is always speaking to us and leading and guiding us. We can trust Him to lead us into cultivating healthy, loving marriages and happy, blessed children and families. I have experienced this in my own life. As long as I listen to that still, small voice and obey what I hear Him saying, the Lord turns every bad situation around in a miraculous way.

Thank God for His Holy Spirit, who is truly an ever present help in time of need. It is reassuring that you don't have to know everything ahead of time. The Holy Spirit is always there to lead you and guide you in everything. If you ever have an issue arise that you don't have an answer for, ask the Holy Spirit. James 1:5 says, *"If any of you lacks wisdom, let him ask of God, who gives to all liberally and without reproach, and it will be given to him."* I know that He is my secret to success as a wife and mother. I knew nothing much at all when I decided to get married and have kids. The Holy Spirit has either taught me what I needed to know through speaking to me directly, or He has led me to the reading material or people who had the information I needed. To have healthy, blessed marriages and families, all we need to do is humble ourselves and ask Him and receive from Him.

Against the Stream

When our children are first born, they are completely innocent. They are completely unaware of the complexities of the world around them. They haven't been exposed to any kind of evil. Unfortunately, as our children grow, their eyes are opened to the imperfections of this world. They see some of the evils that are present.

Some parents believe that it is good to expose their children to negative situations or unkind people. These parents may even be harsh toward their children without comforting them, trying to "toughen them up." However, the Bible paints a different picture.

Romans 16:19 states:

> *For the report of your obedience has reached to all; therefore I am rejoicing over you, but I want you to be wise in what is good and innocent in what is evil.*

> *New American Standard Bible*

And Philippians 4:8 says:

> *Finally, brethren, whatever things are true, whatever things are noble, whatever things are just, whatever things are pure, whatever*

things are lovely, whatever things are of good report, if there is any virtue and if there is anything praiseworthy—meditate on these things.

Studies have shown that if children grow up with a good childhood, feeling safe, loved, and nurtured, they grow up to be well-adjusted adults, able to handle the challenges of life and of raising their own family. That is not a huge surprise to me, and I bet it isn't to you either.

We have seen for ourselves plenty of children who, having grown up in less-than-desirable childhood conditions, repeat the patterns experienced in their childhood. It reminds me of a familiar saying: The apple doesn't fall far from the tree. However, this saying doesn't factor in the redeeming power of God. Any broken life submitted to Him can be turned into a fruitful, beautiful life. Yet that takes time. How much better is it to raise our children to be men and women who have a strong foundation of love and nurturing? When you take the time to parent God's way, He doesn't need to spend years undoing all the pains, bad attitudes, and bad habits of a child's past. Children raised in a loving environment will be able to stand upon the shoulders of their parents' achievements and go even further and higher than their parents did. This should be our goal.

Furthermore, it is also important to treat our kids like they are great. Treat them like they have a high calling from God to fulfill, because they do. Raising them in this way will cause them to believe that they are destined to be great, and they will *be* great because their lives will follow their most dominant thought. Have you heard the phrase "Where the mind goes, the man follows"? It is based on Proverbs 23:7: *"For as he thinks in his heart, so is he."* Can you see how rich and powerful the Word of God is? That is why believers don't need to be afraid of "ruining" our kids. God is on our side, and He has wisdom available for us in His Word. It will be revealed to us by His Spirit, who will lead us and guide us into all truth!

The Bible shows that we can still raise innocent and pure children in a world that is anything but. Yet this doesn't happen by accident. If we parent our children the way the world does, we will get the same results the world gets. We have to stop trying to "fit in" and do things the "normal" way, and decide that we are going to live godly lives and raise our children up to be godly men and women.

There is a saying that goes "Even a dead fish can swim downstream." It doesn't take any effort to go with the flow of the world. However, it does take effort to go against the stream and decide that you want better for your family and your children than what the world is offering. This will look differently to different families. It all depends on your family circumstances and other factors. That is why it is so important to listen to the Holy Spirit and hear what God is saying to you regarding *your* children and *your* situation.

Homeschooling

For my husband and me, the Lord told us to homeschool our children. I was raised in Australia, and I had only heard of one person who was homeschooled. She was a young girl. She informed me at school one day in the seventh grade that she would be leaving school. I asked her what school she was going to. She replied that she wasn't going to any school; she was going to go to school at home. I was amazed and asked her, "Can you do that?" That was the extent of my homeschool knowledge when the Lord placed it upon my heart to homeschool our children.

Our children weren't school age yet, so I had time to research and plan what I was going to do before the time came. It is awesome how, when God asks you to do something, He sends the most timely people into your life to help you. He also helps you find the right information at the right time. When God asks you to do something, He is not expecting you to do it by yourself. That is what His grace is for. He has empowering grace available for you to do everything He has called you to do. What He calls you to do, He equips you to do. So, the Lord sent me people and information to help me begin to homeschool my children.

Homeschooling makes it much easier to guard my children's hearts because I can easily monitor the influences in their lives. I don't try to keep them ignorant. Instead, I share things with them in the most appropriate way for their particular age. I don't have to worry about the world teaching them about sex before they are mature enough to hear about it. Also, they get to hear it the right way, God's way, and not the world's perversion.

If you feel led to send your children to school, then you can be confident that this is the best choice for your family. But make sure that you are being led of the Lord and not just doing it because that's what "everybody else is doing" and it's the "normal" thing to do. Hear God for yourself.

Also, don't be led by fear. You can't be led by fear and by God at the same time. Remember, if God calls you to homeschool your children, He will give you the grace and the help and everything necessary for you to obey His will. God knows best. You don't have to have everything figured out yourself. You only need to obey and trust God that He knows what He is doing.

Guarding Their Hearts

Another way that we guard the hearts of our children is to monitor what they are watching on TV, the games they are playing, and the music they are listening to. Not everything marketed for children is healthy for them to watch. Be led by the Holy Spirit. If you feel a check in your spirit about a certain show, song, or game and don't know why, trust the leading of the Holy Spirit regardless.

We can be confident that if we are obeying that still, small voice and the peace (or lack thereof) in our hearts, our children are going to be protected from the influence of the Enemy. Whatever goes in our ear gates and eye gates goes into our souls and influences us. It becomes a part of who we are. If we want our children to be godly and kind, it won't happen if they have a steady television diet of violence and disrespectful attitudes. Therefore, monitor diligently what your children are exposed to. It will take effort, but your children are worth it.

Sleepover

There is another important area that I need to address, even though I wish I didn't have to. Many people in the world think that it is normal and acceptable to allow their children to sleep over at their friends' homes. If this is something that is offered to your child, make sure that you are led by the peace of God and then err on the side of caution. This is a huge element to guarding the hearts of your children. This is because studies have shown that many times, these are the places where children have been touched inappropriately or been exposed to pornography for the first time. It's just not worth the risk.

Allow your children to have fun, yet with adult supervision. Don't give the Enemy an open door to influence your children negatively or even to attack them. Your kids are young for such a short period. It is better to be safe than sorry. Besides, there are plenty of fun things for them to do that don't require sleeping over.

Relative Danger

Another thing to be aware of is that when a child is molested, it is usually by either a family member or friend. This is surprising to people, and that's why it is such a danger. A lot of the time, parents don't realize that the threat to their child is so close to home. Be aware of this danger and take the necessary steps to ensure that your child is supervised and safe, by listening to the leading of the Holy Spirit. As I said earlier, it will take effort, but how much easier is it to raise a healthy, whole child than to raise one with a broken heart and spirit?

The Power of Your Words

Another vital part of guarding the hearts of your children is watching the words that you speak toward them.

Proverbs 18:21 says:

Death and life are in the power of the tongue:

and they that love it shall eat the fruit thereof.

King James Version

This is absolute truth. Remember that God created the whole world with just the words of His mouth.

Genesis 1:3 (*KJV*) states:

And God said, Let there be light: and there was light.

God also said, in Genesis 1:26-27, that He made us in His image and in His likeness. Therefore, if God created with His words, and we are made in His image and likeness, then we also create with our words.

I cannot emphasize enough the power and impact of a parent's words over and toward their children. Children know that their parents are the most intimately acquainted with them compared to anyone else. Therefore, they will believe everything we tell them about themselves. They will believe that it is truth, even if it is not.

As parents, we need to make sure that every word we speak over our children is in line with who God says they are in His Word. If you don't know what God says in His Word, it is important to get into the Word and find out.

We should we be speaking those truths not only over our children, but also over ourselves. God has given us authority over the children He entrusted to us. Because of this God-ordained order, our words carry more weight with our children. It is important, then, to use this power to speak life, hope, and blessing over and into our children. We need to equip them to move into the fullness of who God created them to be and to ultimately have an intimate relationship with their heavenly Father.

God speaks those things that be not as though they were (Rom. 4:17). That's how He created everything we see today. If there is something we see in our child that needs changing, we don't speak the obvious. If we do that, we are only confirming the facts and not allowing the transforming power of God to work in our child's situation. If we instead speak over them positive affirmations, our child will believe them, and those affirmations will become true in their life.

If I see one of my children do something that is good and shows good character, instead of just keeping silent, I praise them openly. I have noticed that my children become joyful when I do this, and in the future, they make sure that they behave in the same way to be noticed by me. This is because they now believe that this is who they are, and if that is who they are, then that is how they will behave. Besides, they enjoy the positive feedback they receive from me, so they continue that good behavior.

However, if you are consistently highlighting their faults, your children will feel like those negative words are who they are and they will continue to act the same way. If you only notice and give attention to them when they are doing something naughty, then not only will they not do the right thing, they will continue to do the negative behavior in order to get attention from you.

Real-Life Examples

I had a friend who experienced this very thing. His teenage son was constantly acting up and being disobedient and rebellious. My friend did not understand why his son was acting this way. One day, as he was about to correct his son once again, he heard the Lord say, "It's your fault." My friend paused and dismissed himself from the room. He inquired of the Lord as to how this rebellion could be his fault. The Lord revealed to him that he was not giving his son the affection and attention that he needed. Because of it, his son was acting out to get attention from his father. Even though it was negative attention, it was still attention. My friend repented to the Lord and to his son and endeavored to lavish his son with the attention and affection he was craving. My friend's son stopped his rebellious ways.

This experience further illustrates the importance of being balanced toward your children and not neglecting correction, affection, or instruction. All three are needed to raise children to become happy, secure, and content adults.

I recently saw a story on social media. A mother was telling the story of one of her daughters, who was around ten years old. Unlike her other siblings, this daughter was a really sad child. She was having a hard time at school and would often be found looking forlorn and crying. One day her mother had an idea. She decided that every morning while she was doing her daughter's hair for school, she would start speaking positive affirmations over her daughter. So, every morning, for about five minutes, the mother started speaking positive words of affirmation over her daughter. She told her daughter how precious she was, how bright her future was, how much she was loved, and also what the Word of God said about her. Within a short period of time, the whole demeanor of her daughter changed. It was like she was a completely different person. She started smiling and being happy instead of being sad and forlorn. She also started excelling more at school and became really popular among her peers.

As parents, we need to really understand the power of our words toward our children. We can create life with our words, or we can create death. So, speak life to your children. Take every moment to build them up. If they need to be corrected, remind them that the behavior they just displayed is not who they truly are. Then remind them who they really are. Tell them that they are a mighty man or woman of God. Tell them that they are precious, sweet, generous, lovely, patient, etc. When they know who they are, they will manifest that truth. Our lives go in the direction of our most dominant thought. So, if we believe that we are godly, we will respond in a godly way. If we believe that we are useless and can't do anything right, then we will start to manifest that truth.

One example of this is illustrated in the following true story of a friend of a former pastor of mine. My pastor's friend had a son who was a C and D student. He wasn't performing very well at school. My pastor told his friend to have his son confess the following confession over himself every day: "I have favor with God, and I have favor with man. I have wisdom and a good understanding." This young man was diligent to confess this over himself every day. In short order, he went from being a C and D student to an A and B student. As you can see, your confession over your child, and your child's confession over themselves, is very powerful!

In a negative example of this, my husband worked for a very successful man years ago. He was a multimillionaire and graduated at the top of his class at Harvard Business School. However, he was also one of the most miserable men my husband had ever met. This was because while he was growing up in his father's house, his father was extremely critical. Because my husband's boss grew up with a constant flow of criticism, he was always extremely critical of himself. As he was working, he would angrily vocalize things to himself, such as, "You can't do anything right; you're useless!" or "How could you mess that up? You're so dumb! How can you be so (bleeping) stupid?" My husband would see the pain and anguish on this man's face. He would also see that this man would mess up simple tasks over and over again. It was really sad to see that such a successful, grown man with a wife and children was still tormented by words spoken over him decades earlier by his father.

I have heard many, many stories like this. But we can use the power of our words to bless and not to curse. Even if our child has a character trait that is undesirable, it will not help them to overcome it if we keep speaking and reinforcing the obvious. We need to start speaking over them what the Word of God says about them. If they are acting lazy, speak over them that laziness is not who they are, that they are diligent. If they hear it long enough, they will believe it and will manifest it in their character. However, if we say, "You're so lazy! You never do anything!" this will not only be discouraging to our child, but they won't feel empowered to change. It will be a negative cycle. Besides, a negative behavior is not who they are; it is simply what they are doing. So, be sure to reinforce to your child that although they may be exhibiting certain undesirable traits, it is not who they are. Remind them of who they are and who God created them to be. As a parent, you will have positive results by speaking to your child the way that God does and not the way the Enemy does. Remember that the Enemy is the one who is called the accuser of the brethren.

So, be encouraged! The power of change is in your mouth!

Be an Example

Another very important aspect to raising happy kids is the power of our example. Our kids learn way more through what we do than what we say. Our kids are watching us all the time. They look up to us, and whatever they see us do, they think that is normal. We create a culture in our home, and as our children grow, they will adopt a lot of this culture. If that is all they know growing up, then they will just automatically believe it's normal and will apply the same sorts of habits and routines into their adult lives.

For instance, if your parents prayed with you before bed, you believe that this is the normal thing to do and will more than likely pray with your children before bed also. If your parents both sat down at the dinner table as a family with all the children, you would more than likely do the same with your family. Conversely, if your parents ate dinner in front of the TV with very little family interaction, you might not think twice about creating the same culture in your home.

This applies to every area. Your kids are watching how you respond to your husband. Do you honor him with your words and actions, or are you disrespectful? Your children are watching how you interact with others outside the home. Are you cordial in their presence but then speak ill of them as soon as they leave? Your kids are watching all of this.

I don't want anyone to feel condemned or fearful, because none of us are perfect. However, as we realize the importance of developing our relationship with God, He will give us the grace to begin to change many of our actions so that we will be more and more Christlike.

As I mentioned earlier, when my first two kids were little, I was very busy being a mom to them and adjusting to my new role. I loved the Lord, but I did not spend much time with Him or in doing spiritual activities. I wondered to myself, *How are my kids going to know the goodness of the Lord if I don't demonstrate it in my daily walk?* I decided to begin to press in to God again, like I did before they were born. I wasn't always consistent with it, but over the years, I have grown a lot in my relationship with God and also in my character. Now I live out my relationship with the Lord in clear view of my children. They believe that serving and trusting the Lord is normal, even though it is as far from the world's idea of normal as you can get. I don't want to raise my kids to think that the world is normal, but that loving and serving the Lord with your whole heart is.

I am quick to share testimonies of the Lord's goodness with my kids. Every time the Lord answers prayer, I gather the children around me and give a praise report to them of what the Lord has done. This brings me so much joy to do this, and the children rejoice with me also. This builds their faith to know that God is a good Father and that nothing is impossible with Him. My children will eventually have my ceiling as their floor and will build upon the foundation of faith that their father and I have laid for them. That is God's desire for families.

Deuteronomy 6:4-7 says:

Hear, O Israel: The LORD our God, the LORD is one! You shall love the LORD your God with all your heart, with all your soul, and with all your strength. And these words which I command you today shall be in your heart. You shall teach them diligently to your children, and shall talk of them when you sit in your house,

*when you walk by the way, when you lie down,
and when you rise up.*

God wants us to be very vocal with our children and to speak of Him frequently. This is all to help our children develop their own trust relationship with their heavenly Father. After all, what could be more important than that? Many parents focus too much on giving their children plenty of extracurricular activities, buying them the latest toys and gadgets, or putting a great deal of focus on academic achievement. These aren't wrong in themselves, as long as they are in balance and not placed as idols in our lives. Yet what could be more important than where and how our children spend eternity? After everything is said and done, I want my children to know and love the Lord above all else and to spend their eternity in heaven with Jesus. So, make it your focus to show your kids, through your loving actions and words toward them, that God is a good and loving Father.

I had a good and loving father growing up (and I still do), and the way that I saw my father is the same way I saw God. Because of my earthly father, I had no problem believing that God was a good God. I easily believed that God was kind and loving. I had no problem having a trust relationship with the Lord, because I perceived that God must be just like my dad. I am blessed to have the father that I do. God gave us earthly fathers, who we can see, to help us understand our heavenly Father, who we can't see. Unfortunately, not everyone grows up with a loving father. I have a friend whose father used to be very harsh with him and would often violently beat him. The Lord spoke to his heart one day and told him, "I am not like your earthly father. I am more like your mother."

So, as parents, we model the love of God to our

children through our actions, our affection, our correction, and our instruction. This is a high calling, and the Lord has the grace available for us to do it well.

Mark 8:36 says:

> *For what will it profit a man if he gains the whole world, and loses his own soul?*

A Confusing Witness

Another reason it is so important to live godly lives in front of our children is that many children grow up in homes where their parents confessed to know the Lord and yet lived in a manner contrary. This was very confusing to them, and it caused them to doubt God. These children grew up to live completely godless lives and even hated God because of their parents' hypocritical example. It is much better for a child to grow up in a secular home than to grow up in a home where Christ is professed but not lived.

We need to make sure that we are pursuing our own relationship with Christ. If we are spending time with the Lord and being led by His Spirit, we can trust Him to lead us and guide us in every way concerning our children. They will grow up knowing Him themselves and walking in the destiny He has for them. He knows each of our children intimately. What one child needs may be completely different than another. He made us all unique. That is why partnering with the Holy Spirit is so important. He will speak to us every day and will make sure that we pick up on the various needs of our children. Then He will also give us the grace to fulfill those needs.

We are never alone, and we never need to feel

overwhelmed. God is a good Father and helps us to be good mothers and fathers to our children as we lean completely on Him.

I want to reemphasize the importance of pursuing your own personal relationship with God. Most parents in the world raise their children according to their own understanding. Yet Proverbs 14:12 says:

There is a way that seems right to a man, But its end is the way of death.

Also, Matthew 15:14 says:

Let them alone. They are blind leaders of the blind. And if the blind leads the blind, both will fall into a ditch.

Some parents try to figure out for themselves how to raise their kids. They pull from their experience in their own childhood (whether that means doing the same thing or the complete opposite), or they listen to others who don't have a relationship with God. It really is the blind leading the blind. Children are too precious to raise them using trial and error.

I have listened to older mothers who raised their children before they were saved. They listened to the counsel of the world, and they regret not being able to raise their children under the counsel of the Word of God. Their children have already grown up with certain characteristics that are now ingrained in them, characteristics that aren't godly. This has become one of their greatest regrets.

As believers, we don't need to make the mistakes of the world. We know that a child isn't just flesh. A child is an eternal spirit who has a soul and lives in a body. The Bible and the Holy Spirit address all three. You can trust the Word of God to be your guide in raising your children well. The Word is timeless and will always be the answer for how to raise kids well.

So, how do we know what the Word of God says? First, we need to read it, and it needs to be illuminated by the Holy Spirit. If we are not pursuing our own relationship with Jesus, we will be more influenced by the world and the world's way of doing things than by God and His ways. We need to live a lifestyle of relationship with the Lord in order to start adopting His ways of doing things and to have those ways translate into our parenting. If we haven't allowed God to develop patience within us, how can we model and teach patience to our children? If we don't have integrity in dealing with people and money, how can we raise kids with integrity? If we don't know the Lord intimately ourselves, how can we show our kids that He is good? Therefore, it is so vital for us to pursue our own love relationship with the Lord in order to raise our children well.

Let's keep the most important thing as the most important thing and not get swayed by the priorities or pressures of the world and the world's system. We must go against the flow of the world and do things that the world is not doing to get the results that the world is not getting. We need to raise our children to know and love God so they can be happy and secure adults who will raise the next generation well.

IV. Teaching Your Children Obedience

When I only had two children, I wasn't consistent in making sure that they listened to my word, so I got really stressed at times because they would often be disobedient. (This highlights another blessing of well-trained children: When you train your kids to obey, you don't get worn-out, stressed, or angry. The kids get a happier mom!) We would go to church as a family of four and I would rely on my husband to keep the kids in line. This is because although they wouldn't obey me, they would always obey their dad. Will, my husband, had more success than I did because he had no problem backing up his words with necessary correction, whereas I was being lazy about it. Instead of giving the kids the correction they needed when they needed it, I would give them verbal warnings and repeat myself over and over, getting more and more stressed and frustrated because of it.

Even though I felt stressed, I did not make the obvious change until my husband joined the US Army and was about to leave me alone with the kids for a few months to go for training in another state. I knew that I would have to take the kids to church by myself. They would have to listen to me, since their dad wouldn't be around anymore to help. That was the motivation I needed. I stopped slacking and started being consistent with enforcing my words with correction. It did not take very long before they took my word as seriously as they took their dad's. I was able to take them to church by myself, and they were lovely and well behaved. Other church members would stop me to compliment me on how well behaved my children were.

There are three main elements that are vital in raising a child well. If you neglect one of these, your child will grow up lacking for the rest of their lives. Therefore, it is vital for parents to make sure that their children receive all three. These three elements are correction, affection, and instruction.

Correction

Having your children obey your voice is of utmost importance. It is also very important for them to obey you the first time you say something, and to obey you when you are telling them something in a very calm tone of voice. The tone you want to use to have your children obey you in public, at church, or at a friend's home is the tone you will need to use at home to require obedience.

We all train our children one way or another, whether we do it intentionally or not. You are actually the one teaching your children whether or not they have to listen to you the first time. You are teaching them whether they can get away with not obeying your words until you begin counting to three, begin yelling at them, or something else. Therefore, it is vitally important for you to train them to obey your "calm voice" the first time you instruct them to do something. This is so when there is a life-or-death situation, or if you are simply at home or out in public, they will obey your words the first time and every time.

Children don't automatically know how to behave acceptably at church or at a funeral, for example. Therefore, it is important to teach them to obey your calm commands so that you can rest assured that they will be quiet and respectful in sensitive situations and not cause a disturbance to everyone around them. You will be glad you did.

A few years back, my husband was in a classroom full of US Army military policemen. They were all being very vocal about how terrible it was to correct children using the biblical method of the rod of correction. My husband did not agree with them at all. He stood up and gave a personal story that clearly showed the importance of training your children by the rod in a biblical fashion. He showed them that if he and I had not trained our firstborn to obey our voice, she would possibly not be alive today. When he was done with his story, no one spoke a word. They all saw the wisdom in his words and didn't dare say anything contrary again.

He told them about when our firstborn, Kiera, was very young, about two or three years old. She, her dad, and I were out in the front of our house one day, and Will started walking toward a large truck where his friend was waiting for him. Will had to walk onto the street and around to the far side of the truck to get in. Kiera did not realize what was going on and started innocently running after her daddy. She was about to run out onto the street and didn't see a second vehicle driving up quickly and about to pass the truck, threatening to run her over. She was too little to perceive the danger. I saw what was happening and yelled out, "Kiera, STOP!" She immediately stopped running and stood very still. A few seconds later, the vehicle sped by our home without incident. I believe that this was a life-or-death situation. Had I not trained her to listen to my voice, she may not be alive right now. Also, since I trained her to listen to my calm voice, when I raised it out of panic, she obeyed it all the more quickly!

I heard a tragic story about a family who did not train their young daughter to obey them. The family was out and about one day when their daughter started running away from them and into traffic. Her father yelled at her to stop, but she did not listen. Nothing the father said made any difference, and he could not catch up with his daughter before she was struck and killed by an oncoming vehicle.

Practical Tips: Time-Out Method

I don't believe in the time-out method. The time-out method is not biblical. And who knows what our children need more than the One who created them? Besides, if a child doesn't obey their parents, why would they even stay in time-out? I have seen parents stand behind their child and force them to stay in the corner. This does not teach the child to submit themselves to their parents. It gives them time to brood and does not help their heart to choose not to be rebellious. I have seen over and over how children who are "corrected" through the time-out method are just as disobedient as ever.

Recent studies have found that when children are put into time-outs, it teaches them that when they do something wrong or make a mistake, they will be forced to be by themselves. Young children view this as rejection. Furthermore, it communicates to children that their parents only want to be around them when they are doing the right thing, and will cut them off from their presence if they aren't. Misbehavior is sometimes a cry for attention, and if we isolate our kids because of misbehavior, it doesn't help the situation. As you can imagine, it only makes things worse.

Brain imaging has recently shown that brain activity caused by pain of rejection, such as what is perceived by children during time-outs, looks very similar to the brain activity caused by physical pain. However, the use of the rod is swift, and then it is over. After the use of the rod, the parent has the opportunity to immediately show affection to their child and give their child comfort, explaining how the correction can be avoided next time. However, time-outs are experienced for an extended period of time, causing unintended grief.

Time-outs don't even have the desired outcome that parents expect. Instead of making the child calm down and reflect on their behavior, it only causes the child to brood and become even angrier. It makes the process of correction unnecessarily drawn out and ineffective. It is wisdom, therefore, to draw upon the wisdom of God and do what He says in His Word. We can rest assured that He knows best and that we can trust His methods.

My children are outside playing on the trampoline right now. I know without a shadow of a doubt that if I stick my head outside and calmly tell them to come inside, they will all obey immediately. However, we had a little boy come over to play once. His mother is a Christian, yet she felt it was wiser to use the time-out method to "correct" her child.

Her child, "Toby," was playing outside in the snow with my children. When it was time for Toby and his mother to leave, his mother went outside and asked him to come inside. Toby refused and continued to play. His mother pleaded with him over and over to come inside and even gave him the reason why he needed to. It was really awkward for me to stand by and watch this. I can imagine that it felt awkward for this mother also. My children were shocked at the behavior of the child (even though his disobedience was mild compared to many kids). I ended up having to tell my children to come inside. This helped Toby's mother and gave Toby an incentive to come inside himself, since he no longer had anyone to play with. Of course, my children obeyed my words immediately, and then Toby followed with a scowl on his face.

Proverbs 13:24 says:

> *He who spares his rod hates his son, But he who loves him disciplines him promptly.*

And Proverbs 22:15 says:

> *Foolishness is bound up in the heart of a child; The rod of correction will drive it far from him.*

God makes it clear that a little bit of temporary discomfort of the flesh (prompt correction through the use of the rod) is what is needed for the overall benefit of the child. I can tell you from experience that it works.

So, when you give your children an instruction or a command such as "Pick up your toys and put them in the toy box," it is important that you get their full attention and make sure that they know and understand what is required of them. Then, if they disobey your instruction, there needs to be the consequence of the rod. Your kids need to know that your words carry weight and need to be obeyed. They need to know that your instructions and commands aren't just suggestions.

How to Administer the Rod

I spoke to one mother who was constantly running after a crawling baby who was getting into everything she wasn't supposed to. The mother looked at me and said, "I am looking forward to the time when my child can understand reasoning. Then I can explain to her *why* it's wrong, and then she won't do it anymore." The problem with that reasoning, apart from being unscriptural, is that by the time children are old enough to understand the consequences of their actions and even care about those consequences, they have developed many bad habits and attitudes and obviously have been disobedient to their parents for years. It is great wisdom to put aside your thoughts, ideas, and opinions, and stop leaning to your own understanding. Just believe and trust in what God has said in His Word. He is not a man that He should lie (Num. 23:19). It is not holier to withhold the rod and favor the "reasoning" and "time-out" methods of correction. Some parents actually think that they are more virtuous parents because they use these methods of correction instead of the biblical method of the rod. Yet it doesn't take a genius to realize that God's way is the virtuous way to correct your children. It is also the only way to do it correctly. It is truly virtuous to put aside your own ideas and, instead, to trust and submit to what God says.

The Bible clearly states in Proverbs 13:24:

He who spares his rod hates his son, But he who loves him disciplines him promptly.

When any of my children have disobeyed my word, I tell them calmly that they are getting the rod. I lay my child across my lap and not over a bed or couch. It is done in this way to maintain closeness to my child while I am administering correction. This helps to show that I still love and care for them. Once they are in position, I give them one or two swats with the rod on the bottom. It is best to not do it through clothing (and especially not on the outside of a diaper, because they won't feel it). Bare skin is best, yet sometimes I administer a swat on their bottom through their underwear. They normally cry and want a hug immediately, so I give it to them. This is important. They have received their correction and it is over, so affection should not be withheld from them. I then talk to them calmly. I ask them if they know why they got a swat with the rod. They tell me why they think they got a swat. I explain to them why what they did was wrong and how they should respond correctly next time. They understand and go on their merry way, knowing that they have received the correction, and now it is behind them. They also know that they now have a clean slate and can choose to do the right thing next time. That is important. It is also important that they receive affection and instruction after you administer the rod. All three (correction, affection, and instruction) must work together in unison to raise a happy and well-behaved child.

It is also vitally important not to respond to your child's disobedience in anger. Correction must always be administered calmly and with self-control. That is why it is the wisdom of God to use a rod and not your hand. It can be so easy to use your hand and swat your child out of anger and frustration, yet it takes time to go and get the rod to administer correction. Another reason that it's godly wisdom to use the rod is that your child does not learn to shy away from your hand, because you have never had to raise it against them. Your hands are for affection; the rod is for correction. Your children will make a distinction between the two. Also, notice that I am using the word *correction*, not punishment. The rod is for correction. It is used to adjust your child's behavior. It is not meant to punish them.

The Bible uses the word *rod*, but is not specific about the dimensions or the material with which a rod is made. Whatever you feel led of the Lord to use as a rod needs to be effective but not damaging. Test a rod on yourself first so that you know the right amount of force to use to be effective but not damaging. We want to be careful because we never want to abuse our children in any way. I want to reiterate that. Correction is the polar opposite of abuse. Correction is for the benefit of the child and is administered with self-control and love. Abuse is the Enemy's counterfeit to godly correction. It is done with a lack of self-control and with anger and self-centeredness. It is because parents have abused their children in this way that even godly correction is now frowned upon in society. So, don't equate the two and thereby reject the godly way of correcting your children. God's way will bear good fruit in your child's life. You can trust God on that!

Your child will probably cry after you correct them with the rod. That is normal. If your child remains emotionless or unmoved after you have administered the rod, then you may not have administered the rod effectively and may need to reapply it.

Daddy and Obedience

One good thing to remember is that threatening your children with "Just wait until your daddy gets home!" prolongs the correction. It causes your child to possibly have to wait hours for their father to return home and administer correction. This can be tormenting for the child, and it is unbiblical. We have seen from Proverbs 13:24 that correction must be administered promptly. There is great wisdom in this. Besides, the last thing your husband wants to do when he gets home from work is administer correction to his children. He wants his return home from work to be a joyful experience for his children, not a feeling of dread. Mothers, you have the authority and the grace to correct your children promptly like the Bible states. It is better for you, your child, and your husband.

To be clear, I am not saying that the father of your child doesn't help correct them. When he is around and witnesses your child in disobedience, he must administer that correction himself. For the ultimate health of the child, it is important that both parents be consistent, in agreement, and in unity.

As parents, it is important that we place our own spiritual health and the spiritual health of our family as the top priority. To be promoted in God's kingdom, we need to be faithful with who and what God has given us. When we have our family and home in order, God knows that we can be trusted with much more. The Scripture confirms this in 1 Timothy 3:4-5, where it talks about the qualities and attributes needed by a man before he is put into a position of authority in the church: *"One who rules his own house well, having his children in submission with all reverence (for if a man does not know how to rule his own house, how will he take care of the church of God?)"* This just goes to show the importance of pouring into your own family and children first. Promotion comes from the Lord, and what you do in secret will be rewarded openly. When you spend the necessary time and effort to diligently teach, train, and correct your children in your home, the fruit of it will be evident to all when you step outside into the public eye.

I recently read about one mother's reasoning for not using the rod of correction. She said that she didn't want to use that method anymore because she didn't want to teach her daughter that it was okay to hit. This is, once again, an example of man deciding that they know better than God. However, it is better to trust God's Word and to do what He says than to decide to do your own thing. God is infinitely wiser than we are, and we are better off doing what He says than trying to figure it out on our own. Many have realized days, months, or years down the road that God was right and they should've listened to His counsel in the first place. But by then, it was too late.

Besides, I am not advocating using our hands to "hit." The Bible tells us to use the rod—not our hands—to correct our children. If we adhere to what God says, we can be assured of the best outcome for the children who have been entrusted into our care by our loving Father.

When to Begin Training

When do you know your child is old enough to start training?

It is best to train your children as early as possible, as soon as they understand right from wrong. If you do the training early, then the older they get, the less and less you have to use the rod. By the time your children are preteens, the rod becomes unnecessary and mostly ineffective. By that time, your children already know what is required of them and already have a heart to do what is right. At that point, all that is necessary is verbal correction and, at times, a revocation of privileges.

This is another area where the Holy Spirit will lead and guide you. All children are different, and some develop in their understanding faster than others. The Holy Spirit will give you wisdom and will show you when your child understands what you are saying and is choosing to do the wrong thing anyway. You can even see it in their actions.

For instance, let's say that you've told your child in the past not to touch something. They decided to do so anyway, but before they went to touch it, they looked at you to see if you were going to do anything about it. It is obvious that they know that they are doing the wrong thing, and it shows that they are ready to be corrected. There will be other cues too, but just be led by the Holy Spirit. Each child is an individual, and the Lord knows when the right time is to train your child.

One day I was breastfeeding my daughter, who was about seven months old at the time, and she started having a tantrum in my lap for no good reason. I was trying to latch her onto my breast, and she was arching her back and being very vocal. I was trying to give her what she wanted, yet she was resisting my efforts. I thought to myself, *Surely she is too young to know what she is doing.* But I decided to see. I gave her a little swat on the leg and firmly and calmly said, "No." Sure enough, she settled right down, latched on to drink, and never did that again.

I have never had to worry about my nursing child

pulling the nursing cover off me and exposing me, because they learned to listen to the word *No* or *Stop.* I regularly saw other mothers struggle in a power play with their babies, toddlers, and children. I never had their problems. It wasn't that my children were special. It was because I trusted God's Word and implemented what it said, which produced obedient and joyful children. The same thing is available to any and all who will put priority on God's Word and simply do what He says. It's simple. It just comes down to our choice.

Baby Boot Camp #1

When my children were old enough to start crawling around the home and exploring and touching things that were off limits or potentially harmful to them, I started doing an intentional training time, a "baby boot camp." This can be done by placing something on the table that your child is interested in but is not allowed to touch. This might be food, sunglasses, the television remote, or a drinking glass. You calmly tell your child not to touch it. You point to it and say calmly, "Don't touch." As they reach out to touch it, you give them a quick swat with the rod on the meaty part of their thigh and simultaneously say firmly and calmly, "No. Don't touch." (It is not good to swat your child on the hand, because there isn't much fat on the top of the hands, and you don't want to damage your child.) Once you do this, they normally stop what they're doing immediately and process what just happened. Then they normally go to reach out for it again, so you have to repeat the process again.

What happens is that your child begins to associate the words *No* and *Don't touch* with discomfort. You will only need to repeat this process a few times before they stop trying to touch whatever it was you placed on the table. When you see that your child is obeying your word, it is extremely important to lavish them with praise and a huge smile. After you have trained your child in this way, when they reach out to touch something they are not allowed to touch, all you have to say is "No" or "Don't touch" and your child will stop trying to touch it and will move on. (Always remember to praise them for their obedience.) I'm telling you, it's that simple. And it works. If, after a while, they decide to be disobedient and touch it anyway, you need to reinforce your words with the rod again. If you're not consistent, and if your child knows that they can get away with it sometimes, they will take the chance and try it every time. If you haven't been consistent for a season, just make it a focus to be consistent every time. It won't be long before they learn that you mean what you say and that disobedience will yield consequences.

If your children are already older and have been rebellious for a long time, it might take more time and effort, but if you're consistent, it won't take too long. It only takes two or three days to train your child out of disobedient behaviors.

Just to be clear, when your children are little, you don't have to use much force when you administer the rod during training. When I trained my little ones, they never once cried, any of them. It just wasn't necessary to use much force to get my point across. So, that goes to show how simple and effective this is. You don't need to be timid or to put off training your little ones. It is good for them, and it is good for you.

Proverbs 22:15 says:

Foolishness is bound up in the heart of a child;

The rod of correction will drive it far from him.

A Note for Older Children

For older children who are already old enough to understand instruction, you do not need to set up an intentional training time; you just need to make sure that they know their boundaries and what is expected of them. Make it clear to them so that there is no confusion. Then, if they decide to step outside those boundaries or show disobedience in other ways, it is important to follow through with correction by the rod. Once they've experienced that you now back up your words with correction, they will understand that what was acceptable in the past is no longer acceptable, and they will change their behavior.

There are a lot of mothers who are very stressed and running after their kids all day. My life could easily be the same, but I have chosen to simply train my children to listen to my words, and they do. I don't have to run after them, and you don't either.

As I said, I normally start to train my children before they can walk. One time I was at a friend's home and was sitting on the couch, surrounded by other people. Kiera, my firstborn, was crawling at the time. She was in the living room with me, but she was on the other side of the coffee table. She started crawling to our host's sound system, which was lying on the floor. I simply said, "Kiera, no." Kiera immediately stopped crawling toward it, sat straight up, and changed course. She started crawling in a different direction, knowing that she wasn't allowed to touch the sound system. It did not take much time or effort to get her to that place of obedience. I was amazed at how simple and effective just a few minutes of intentional baby boot camp was.

Baby Boot Camp #2

Another way you can train your child to be obedient is to train them to sit still and patiently in your lap. This is a good discipline for them to have.

Start by sitting them squarely in your lap. When they start to shift their legs to get down or start arching their back, quickly say, "No." Follow that with a swat of the rod on their thigh and then place them squarely back in your lap. They may whine or complain, but hang in there. If you quit before they obey, you will only have taught them that if they try hard enough or long enough, they can have their own way. It may take a few minutes of consistency, or it may take many minutes. The point is, no matter how long it takes, don't let them off your lap until they obey. When they obey, make sure you shower them with praise! Sometimes when you praise them, they'll think that they can get off your lap. So, don't get thrown off by this. Keep them on your lap until they are clearly obeying and until *you* have initiated that it is okay for them to get down.

Once you have established obedience in some areas, it flows into other areas. Once your children know that they must obey your word, they will obey it, even if it is in an area where they have not been specifically trained.

It is important for you to cultivate patience in your children. Patience is waiting with a good attitude. You are not doing your children any favors by giving them exactly what they want, when they want it. Don't allow them to be impatient or rude. Coach them day after day about the right way to respond in certain situations. Be sure to praise them openly when you see them displaying godly attitudes and behaviors. This is crucial. When they see that their well-doing is not overlooked, this will only reinforce their desire to keep doing good things.

Baby Boot Camp #3

Here is something else that's helpful. If you have two siblings fighting over something, such as a toy, here is a rule of thumb: Whatever they seek to gain, they lose. This means that if your children are being unkind to each other and fighting over a toy, then they both lose the toy. Neither one gets it. This is important, because they were both displaying selfishness. To reward one with the toy would only send the message that this kind of behavior is okay to get what one wants.

Of course, it is always important to take into consideration the ages of the children. If an older child were to take a baby toy away from a young toddler, it would be okay to give the toy to the toddler. However, as the toddler grows, they will need to be taught that they cannot have whatever they want simply by loudly complaining. The Holy Spirit will lead you and will let you know when the time has come.

It is very important to stay consistent with your children. You have to make sure that you back up your word and not get lax about it. Children learn what they can get away with, and if you stop giving them correction for something, they'll know they can get away with it. Then you'll have to train them out of it. It is easier just to stay consistent in the first place. When I say it's easier, I don't mean that it's easy. It definitely takes effort, and that's why a lot of people prefer not to do it.

Baby Boot Camp #4

You can also teach your child to be quiet when you tell them to be quiet. You say "Hush" or "Shhh" and then show them what that means by putting two fingers over their lips. (Make sure that they understand you and are old enough to understand you.) Then, if they continue to talk, give them a swat on the thigh with the rod and repeat your command. Continue this until they obey you. If you give up, they will know that they don't have to listen to you. So, don't give up. They will realize that it is in their best interest to obey. I have taught my kids to be quiet on command. It comes in handy when we are on airplanes, in church, in the car, or when someone is on the phone. That's a big deal! We have taken international flights together as a large family, and people are amazed when they see my kids. Some even say, "I didn't know that there were kids on this flight!"

Baby Boot Camp #5

In the home, I make sure that not only are my children's actions correct, but also their attitudes. Children need to be taught to have thankful and joyful attitudes. If I tell my children to do something, but they do it with a bad attitude, I correct that right away. You can usually spot a bad attitude by such things as slumped shoulders, a scowl on the face, or a negative tone in the voice. If you fail to correct a bad attitude, then you can expect to see more of the same type of behavior. Negative attitudes need to be corrected as soon as they arise.

I was on the phone with a friend once, and she heard me ask my children to do something (I don't remember what it was). She told me that she was jealous of me because my kids just obeyed my commands immediately and with good attitudes. She told me that her kids sighed mournfully when they were asked to do something, and they would wail, "Aww, do I *have* to?" It was a daily battle for her. Yet my kids are not some exception to the rule. I have simply followed what the Bible teaches, and I am getting great results. These results are available to every parent.

It is important to note that some kids are more stubborn than others. My firstborn is very meek and gentle. She obeys quickly and easily. My third child, however, has been my most challenging. She is six now, and I have put time, love, and effort into training and correcting her. You can tell that her heart has softened, and she is not rebellious anymore. She is a delight to be around now, but she was challenging for years!

I have helped cultivate a right attitude in my children. I do not allow them to be ungrateful. Be sure to watch over the attitudes of your children's hearts, and make attitude adjustments if necessary. Your children's attitudes are more important than their actions, because attitude reveals the heart.

Dana Bellamy

V. Why Teach Obedience?

When you make the effort to teach your child to listen to your words right from the beginning, your life will be so much easier in the long run. And so will your child's life. They will know their boundaries, and they will feel more secure and happy because of it. They will come to know that you will be true to your word and that they can trust you.

This makes for happier kids, because they know that "all is well" between you and them as long as they honor the boundaries that you have set for them. They never have to be cautious to carefully monitor your moods, not knowing if you are going to "blow up" or not. Besides, if you train them the right way and train them early, you will never get to the point where you feel like blowing up. If you see them being disobedient, you will simply and calmly administer correction.

This is especially important when your children are close together in age. One day you will be breastfeeding (or bottle-feeding) your baby, unable to reach your toddler who is about to do something dangerous (for instance). Yet if you have already trained your toddler well, all you will have to say is "Stop!" "No!" or "Don't touch!" and they will obey you. You won't have to worry about them getting into everything and tearing up your house while you are sitting down and unable to do anything about it. This is because they will already know the boundaries established for them. Anything new that comes up will only require a simple calm command from you.

We went to a Thai restaurant with all six kids a few weeks back. I can only imagine what the other patrons were thinking when they saw so many kids walk through the door. They probably believed that their peace and tranquility were shattered for sure! But their fears were quickly dispelled when they witnessed how quiet, sensible, and well behaved my kids were. One of the patrons, as he was about to walk out of the restaurant, commented to Will and me, "I couldn't leave without letting you know how amazingly your kids are behaving!"

Another time, a lady ran after us to compliment us on how well behaved she thought our kids were, especially compared to the other children that were also in the overflow room at a college graduation ceremony. I could tell story after story about things like this.

I have also found that my kids benefit from their good behavior in public settings. Many strangers have wanted to bless my children with gifts just because they were blessed by witnessing their behavior.

For instance, when we moved to Colorado from Australia, we flew from Sydney to California on a military flight. The first leg of the flight was from Richmond, Australia, to the island of Guam. We were the only people on the plane apart from the crew. When we landed in Guam, one of the crew members on the flight approached us with US Air Force patches for each of our children. He said sincerely to Will and me, "I have been flying for twenty-five years, and I have never witnessed children who were as well behaved as yours."

Another time we were in a store buying cell phones. The process of starting a new phone service and buying phones turned out to be lengthy. Yet the whole time, my children never complained or misbehaved. The store manager was so impressed that he let each of my children pick out a display phone (that the store no longer needed) to take home as a gift. My kids were so blessed to each have their own "cell phone" like their parents. They would never have received this blessing if they had misbehaved in the store.

When I went to Germany on a Bible college missions trip, Will took the kids grocery shopping and then to Burger King. He told me that there was an older couple at Burger King who were so blessed by our kids' good behavior that the wife purchased each of them an ice cream for dessert. The kids were blessed by that too, of course.

I am not sharing these stories for any other reason than to encourage you. We have seen so much of the "norm" of society in grocery stores and other public places. More often than not, children are being completely disobedient to their parents and creating a scene. However, this is not the "norm" according to God. Society has gotten away from the biblical teaching of administering the rod of correction, thinking that they know better. Yet no one is smarter than God. We can trust Him with our kids.

I have never had to worry about my children throwing tantrums or screaming out in public, because they know they aren't allowed to do that in the home. If they ever throw themselves down in a tantrum at home, I promptly pick them up and administer the rod. Therefore, it never happens more than once, because it isn't tolerated. I know with full confidence that I can tell my children "No" when they ask for something in the store and they will not scream or cry about it. (And with six kids, I have to say "No" a lot!) So, since my children respond well when I tell them "No," I delight in telling them "Yes!" I love to give them treats and gifts because they bring me much joy through their obedience and good attitudes. Now, they are not always obedient or displaying good attitudes, so I still continue to correct them as we go. I praise God that they are obedient and display good attitudes most of the time.

I want to briefly refer to children with disabilities, such as autism, which seems to be more and more prevalent in society. I do not want the mothers of these children to feel like I am not being compassionate about their situation. I know that your situation is different. My experience is just with *my* children, so I am basically referring to children without those disabilities. I would recommend that you seek God on what to do for your specific child and your specific situation. God is also a Healer. I have heard miraculous stories of God completely healing autism. So, be encouraged!

Another "fruit" of raising up obedient children is that I have never had to make different meals for all my kids. I also never have to worry about whether my kids will eat the meals that I prepare for them. I make one meal, and my children are required to eat it. My children know that they have to eat the food that is put in front of them, and they don't give me any issues about it. When they are younger, they may test me and try to get out of eating certain foods.

However, I show them very quickly that they are not allowed to be picky or fussy. They are required to eat the healthy, tasty food that I lovingly prepare for them.

Because of this stance, my children are not picky eaters. They will eat what I put in front of them. They even love to eat all sorts of vegetables and salad. They will even ask for seconds. I was thinking this morning that no matter what meal I cook for my kids, they all like it and ask me if I can make it again sometime. I love that!

Word of Encouragement

If you are not experiencing obedience and good attitudes in your home right now, don't feel bad or condemned about it. I was blessed to come across the information about how to instill these qualities into my children when I was pregnant with my firstborn. When I got the revelation of how to effectively train my children, I tried to follow it right from the start. I was amazed at how simple it was and how much sense it all made. Yet I was also amazed that if I had not come across the information when I did, I would not have figured it out for myself. That's why it is so important for older women to teach the younger, as it states in Titus 2:3-5. We are all born as infants into this world, and we learn as we go. So, if we are not taught something, then how can we do what we have not learned to do?

My experience with training my children according to God's Word is just one example of how beautiful it can be when we do things God's way and trust Him for the outcome. It does not matter if you have rarely (or never) exercised your authority over your kids before. Be encouraged that you can begin training and correcting them through the wisdom and counsel of the Holy Spirit, and you can get your kids on track. You can—and will—have testimonies like these for yourself.

There is a saying that goes "Train them till you like them." And it's so true. I hear mothers complain about their children and talk about how they love them more when they're asleep (because their children are not up to anything naughty when they're asleep). They look forward to when school is in session, and they dread school holidays because they have to be around their disobedient children all the time. This is tragic! Spend the time training your kids to obey, and you will love to be around them. My kids are a joy to be around!

I have already said that it is important to stay consistent. If you're not consistent with your kids, and if they know that they can get away with it sometimes, they will try to get away with it every time!

When Kiera and Jerome were little (and they were my only two kids), they were slamming the door in their bedroom. I was worried that one of them would slam their fingers in the door, so I wanted them to stop. They were also messing with our blinds. I wanted them to stop doing that because I didn't want them to break the blinds. Sometimes I would give them a swat with the rod when they did either of those things, and other times I got lazy and just told them verbally to stop. Since I wasn't consistent, they kept on going. They didn't stop. Like I said, if children can get away with it sometimes, they will try to get away with it every time. The situation was making me mad. (It's important not to act out of anger. That's why it's such sound wisdom to correct your kids before you get to that point.) I read that you can train your kids out of any bad behavior in just three days by being consistent. So, I made a point to not be lazy, but to correct them with the rod every time they did either of those things. I found that after just two days of consistency, they stopped doing both of them altogether. It was awesome.

Heart Motives

Any teaching on the correction of children is incomplete without addressing their heart motives. I cannot emphasize this enough. What I mean by 'heart motives' is the *intention* behind what your child does. Let me explain.

Let's say that you and your child are sitting at the dinner table. While reaching for the salt, your child accidentally knocks over their glass of milk and spills it everywhere. You might find this really frustrating, but this would not be a time for correction by the rod. You might tell your child to be more careful next time, but if you respond in anger and/or correct them by the rod over this, it would be unjust. It was not in your child's heart to disobey you or cause any grief. If you were to correct them because of this, your child would think it was unjust, and you could give them a heart wound. When your child knowingly disobeys you or has done something wrong and gets corrected for it, they know in their heart that the correction was just. This would not be the case if they innocently or unknowingly did something clumsy such as spill a glass of milk.

In the above example, to ascertain whether your child's motives were pure, you would have to listen to the Holy Spirit and use your discernment. If you told them not to touch the salt in the first place, and their reaching for the salt in disobedience is what caused the milk to spill, then correction by the rod would be warranted. It is important, as I have mentioned earlier, not to respond in anger toward your child, even when they spill milk everywhere and you have to clean it up. I know that it is easier said than done, but the Holy Spirit has the grace available for you to mother with excellence. I will talk more about this later.

Story Time

When my first two were still little and I was pregnant with my third, I had terrible morning sickness, so I had to lie down a lot. The kids took advantage of this and started doing wild things that they wouldn't normally do. I saw footprints on our glass dining table one day, and the kids ripped paper homeschool letters and numbers off the walls. It was unbelievable to me! They had never behaved this way before. I then witnessed them doing a naughty thing that they had never done before. Since they had never done it before, I let them off with a verbal warning. Then they did something else uniquely naughty, and I again let them off with a verbal warning. The problem was, the naughtiness never stopped. They just kept finding more unique ways to be naughty! I realized that, regardless of how ill I felt, I needed to stop what I was doing and administer proper correction the very next time they did something naughty. After I started doing that, all the naughtiness quickly stopped and everything went back to normal. What a relief!

The problem was, even though I never expressly told them that they couldn't do those naughty things, it would've been common sense not to do them. I could tell that their hearts weren't in the right place; they were just intent on testing their boundaries. If they had done something by accident, not knowing that it was wrong, that would've been a different story.

There's no need to worry or fret, for the Lord will make the intentions of your child's heart clear to you, and He will help you teach and train them individually. There are many different scenarios that will arise with each of your children. I will not even attempt to cover all the scenarios, because it would be impossible. Besides, I am not here to take the place of the Holy Spirit. The Holy Spirit will take the foundational information that I have given you and will lead you and guide you in every situation that comes up. You can trust His Word and His leading.

The Scripture says in Colossians 3:15, *"And let the peace of God rule in your hearts."* This word *"rule"* is used like an umpire would rule a sports game. So, here's how we could read this verse: "And let the peace of God *act as an umpire* in your hearts." This means that you can know the direction to take and what's right or wrong based on the peace, or lack thereof, in your heart. If you allow the Holy Spirit to lead you through His peace, you can be confident in His leading, and you can't go wrong while obeying it. When you feel His peace in your heart, the Holy Spirit is giving you a "green light" that you are heading in the right direction or doing the right thing. If you start to feel an unrest or a lack of peace in your heart, this is the Holy Spirit giving you a "red light," a gentle warning to stop what you are doing or not head in a certain direction.

Apologizing for Mistakes

Let's say that you made a mistake and corrected your child, only to find out that their intentions were pure and you ended up hurting their heart. I have been in this position myself. We all live and learn. In this case, it is important to humble yourself before your child. Let them know that you are sorry and that you realize that they didn't mean to do what they did. Children are quick to forgive. Then you both can hug and move on.

This leading of the Holy Spirit will really be key as you raise your children. He wants you to raise them so they will grow up to be faithful men and women of God who can be trusted with shepherding the lives of others into His kingdom. God wants your children to know Him, hear His voice, and fulfill their unique destinies. He gave your particular children to you because He has equipped you and given you the grace to shepherd their hearts and lives with excellence. You will do great! I know it!

Here is a real-life example: There was ten-year-old girl in Australia whose mother asked her to hang wet clothes on the clothesline to dry. (In Australia, most people hang their clothes out to dry on clotheslines.) This particular clothesline was suspended in the air on a pole and had four quadrants. The young girl obediently started hanging up the clothes. In her innocence, she thought it would be a really good idea to hang up all the clothes on one quadrant instead of spreading them out across all four quadrants.

She happily completed her task and then proudly showed her mother what she had done. Her mother, standing alongside her, was less than impressed. She promptly slapped the young girl across the back of the head and yelled at her. In angry tones, the mother pointed out that not only was the clothesline now leaning to one side, but the wet clothes wouldn't be able to dry because they were bunched together. Crushed, the young girl realized that her idea wasn't the best. With tears in her eyes and a broken heart, she went to fix her mistake by spreading the clothes out.

What broke the young girl's heart was her mother's harsh response. The mom could have acknowledged the "great feat" accomplished by her daughter, lovingly explained the problem with it, and then kindly asked her to spread the clothes out. The daughter would've happily fixed her mistake, without receiving a broken heart in the process. At the very least, the mother should have apologized to her daughter for not handling the situation in the best way. Unfortunately, this never happened. The child kept this hurt in her heart, not really knowing any better, into adulthood, like many do. Praise be to God that He helped her forgive her mother, and He healed her heart.

I have noticed that if you hold grudges against your parents for certain things they do, you will find yourself doing the same things to your children. Holding unforgiveness against one or both of your parents ends up trapping you in the same pattern of behavior. Do yourself and your children a favor and forgive your parents and release them. This will also release *you* from repeating the same mistakes.

Another thing I have learned is that motherhood isn't easy. I don't want my kids holding grudges against me, especially when I am doing the best I can and sacrificing so much to be there for them and to raise them well. So, treat your parents the same way you want your kids to treat you. Show your parents the same grace that you would want your children to extend toward you. That really helps when you need to forgive your parents. It will bear much fruit in your own family. Offense is deadly. Don't allow it to linger. Draw on the grace of God to forgive as soon as possible.

Bedtime Training

So many mothers have a hard time getting their kids to go to sleep. I don't have that problem. If my children aren't obeying me by lying down and at least attempting to go to sleep, I go into their rooms and correct them with the rod. They soon learn what is expected of them.

As for how I get my babies to sleep through the night, I do not sleep-train my babies after they're born like some mothers try to do. I feed them on demand whenever they need food. Babies need to eat regularly throughout the day and night, and they normally wake up to feed when they are hungry. Since infants go through regular growth spurts where it seems like they are always trying to feed, I don't expect them to sleep through that. Every time I attempted something like that, I was met with frustration. During the normal course of time, I have noticed that my babies wake up less and less for feeds as they get older. Eventually they start sleeping through the night on their own.

If your children never get to a point where they sleep through the night, but wake up to comfort-feed for months on end, ask the Holy Spirit for wisdom. If they are old enough, it may be time to encourage them to sleep through the night.

It boils down to just enforcing what you expect your children to do. They are looking to you for direction. The Holy Spirit will help you set boundaries for your children that are age-appropriate and full of wisdom.

Sometimes new situations arise where I don't know the best course of action to take. Instead of trying to figure it out, I simply take it to the Lord in prayer. The Lord gives me the wisdom in every situation that I face. He always has an answer. Learn to rely on Him and His wisdom instead of trying to parent on your own. The Lord wants to help you at all times and is just waiting for you to ask. It is also important to come into agreement with your husband. There are many times when the Lord has given my husband the answer instead of me. We work together as a team to parent our children and train them.

Just as a reminder, it is of vital importance to balance all training with affection and praise! Don't just give them attention when they do something *wrong*. Give them attention when you see them doing the *right* thing. Think of many ways to praise them throughout the day, and they won't want to be disobedient toward you. They will want to continue to get the praise from you.

Showing physical affection is something that doesn't come easily for all of us. For me, it is very easy to lavish my infants with physical affection, yet as they begin to grow out of that baby phase, it doesn't feel as natural for me to give them kisses and hugs anymore. It is the same for my husband. Yet we both realize the importance of showing physical affection toward our children, so we have sought the Holy Spirit on how to remedy this. He has given us ideas for our family, and He will also give you ideas for yours if this is something that you struggle with.

For instance, the Lord gave me the idea of giving my older children a hug in the morning when they get up and a hug right before they go to bed. What a great way to wake up and go to sleep each day! For my husband, he makes an effort to give each child a hug before he heads out to work. My husband also tickles the younger children because they love it so much. They just laugh and laugh!

In church one day, my pastor shared something he

learned while his children were still young. He learned that some men turn to homosexuality because they never received the physical touch they craved from their fathers. Because of this, these men look for that fatherly affection in all the wrong places.

For this reason, my pastor made a point of having frequent friendly wrestling matches with his son as he was growing up. He would grab his son and they would roll on the living room floor together. His son would be smiling from ear to ear and yelling, "Stop, Dad! Stop!" But what he really meant was, "This feels so good, Dad. I feel so loved." This was especially important for my pastor's son, because his love language was physical touch. There would have been much damage done if my pastor had not gone out of his way to show his son love in the love language that he understood and craved. His son is happily married today.

Some men who have been deprived of physical affection from their fathers will delve into pornography, searching in all the wrong places for what they are lacking.

Similarly, many daughters who have lacked affection from their fathers will grow up looking for attention and affection in relationships with men. They'll often find themselves in unhealthy relationships, trying to fill the void that was left by their earthly fathers. But now that they are adults, it is a void only God can fill.

Therefore, it is vitally important for us to do what is best for our children, and even if we don't feel like it, we need to go out of our way, partnering with Holy Spirit, to give our children the affection they need. If we do this, they won't grow up with this need unfulfilled.

Note to Single Mothers

For those who may be single mothers, I don't want you to feel helpless because you cannot give your children the fatherly affection that they need. God knows what your children have need of. Don't worry about it. Instead, take it to your heavenly Father in prayer. He will send your children what they need as you trust Him to supply. He may use a close family member such as a grandfather to fulfill that role. Maybe even a godly man at church will have it laid on his heart to be a father figure to your children. God will sort it out. But don't be moved by panic or fear. Let the Lord bring the right men into your children's lives. You don't want to act hastily and allow a father figure who was not sent by God. This could be very detrimental. Only God knows the hearts of men, and He will send you one or more with pure motives toward your children.

I once had my pastor and his wife come over to share a meal with my family. My pastor mentioned to me how impressed he was that my kids were always happy. (He was not the first one to say this to me. Others had said the same thing. I had wondered why they hadn't commented on how well behaved my children were but rather how happy they were.) My pastor went on to explain that he had seen children before who were very well behaved, but it seemed as if something was wrong. It seemed as if they did not obey their parents out of a willing, joyful heart, and it seemed as though their spirits were broken. He went on to say, "That is what happens when you correct children to be obedient, but don't balance it with the love, affection, and praise that they need." He noted that I had found a happy balance, as evidenced by my children, and he mentioned that I should write a book. It's funny, but I never considered it back then. Yet here I am!

I also can see, in retrospect, how important it is to examine a child's heart motives. When children are loved and given affection, as well as corrected and instructed in life matters, they will grow up to be well-rounded, secure individuals who will raise happy, content children of their own.

I want to encourage you to take this message to heart. Search the Scriptures and see for yourself what God says about it. I will add a few more scriptures at the conclusion of this chapter. Now that you have heard, it is up to you to either put it into practice or maintain the status quo. If you choose to put God's wisdom into practice, it is important that you do it wholeheartedly. You cannot apply it only part of the time, or it will lead to frustration and disorder in the home. It has to be all or nothing. What do you have to lose? God's Word is truth, and you can trust Him that your children will flourish when you correct them according to His Word.

For mothers-to-be who are reading this book, you have a clean and fresh slate. Teach your kids to be obedient right from the beginning and you will want many children because they bring you so much joy!

For mothers who already have children, don't feel overwhelmed. The Holy Spirit is with you. He will give you the grace you need and will lead and guide you into establishing a home with well-behaved and happy children. Begin by making sure that your children understand whatever instructions or commands you give them, and then back up those instructions and commands with immediate praise or correction. Show your kids that Mom means business, and stay consistent. You will have the results that the Bible says.

Depending on the age of your children, you may feel the Lord leading you to sit them down for a meeting. Humble yourself before them and explain to them what the Bible says about the matter. Repent to them for not doing things the scriptural way up until then. Explain that it is better for them that you implement this in your family. Then don't look back; only look forward. You've got this!

Your children will begin to appreciate and respect the boundaries you have set and enforce. It will be well with their souls.

Here are more scriptures from the Bible to encourage you further:

Proverbs 29:17: *"Correct your son, and he will give you rest; Yes, he will give delight to your soul."*

Proverbs 13:24: *"He who spares his rod hates his son, But he who loves him disciplines him promptly."*

Proverbs 23:13: *"Do not withhold correction from a child, For if you beat him with a rod, he will not die."*

Proverbs 29:15: *"The rod and rebuke give wisdom, But a child left to himself brings shame to his mother."*

Ephesians 6:4: *"And you, fathers, do not provoke your children to wrath, but bring them up in the training and admonition of the Lord."*

Proverbs 22:6: *"Train up a child in the way he should go, And when he is old he will not depart from it."*

Proverbs 22:15: *"Foolishness is bound up in the heart of a child; The rod of correction will drive it far from him."*

Isaiah 54:13: *"All your children shall be taught by the LORD,*

Dana Bellamy

And great shall be the peace of your children."

VI. Marriage

Marriage is the foundation of the home. A happy family is built upon the foundation of a happy marriage. This book wouldn't be complete without my sharing some of the things I have learned within my own happy marriage.

Children learn what is acceptable and normal by watching how their father treats their mother. If their father is very loving, respectful, and protective of their mother, it teaches a daughter what to expect from a future husband and to not settle for anything less. It also teaches a son how to treat a future wife. In the same way, it is important for a mother to model what it is to be a godly wife toward her husband. As your children see you being a godly helpmeet to your husband, treating him with respect in word and deed, they will know how to behave when they are married, or what a godly wife looks like. You will set them up for successful marriages.

As a young woman, I heard many stories of husbands dreading going home to their wives for one reason or another. A majority of the time, it was because of strife within their marriages. It always bothered me to hear about this, and I have always said to myself, *I want to be a wife that my husband **wants** to come home to.* And I have endeavored to be just that. Proverbs 25:24 (*NIV*) says, *"Better to live on a corner of the roof than share a house with a quarrelsome wife."* My husband and I have disagreements or conflicts here and there, just like anybody else. However, I strive to be a godly wife to my husband and to create a peaceful sanctuary in our home. He considers me his best friend, as I do him. His favorite thing to do is to spend time with me, and that blesses me so much. Sure, he likes to also go fishing, since it is a passion of his, but he makes sure that his fishing time is balanced with his family time. He knows that we are his first priority.

I am not saying that everything has to be perfect at home all the time, but even when an issue arises, we have a *choice* about how to respond to it. No one can *make* us do anything against our will, at least on a heart level. We are the ones who *choose* how we will respond to every situation in life. We can choose to be carnally minded and respond in the flesh, or we can choose to be spiritually minded and respond in the Spirit, trusting God for the outcome.

I am also not saying that we can never have disagreements, only that the disagreements must be resolved in a respectful way. Sometimes when I am having a conflict in my marriage, I just pray, "Lord, help!" The Lord then quickly turns the situation around. But I need to partner with and obey the Holy Spirit. If He tells me to humble myself and apologize to my husband for my part in the conflict, I need to do it. I like to resolve conflict as soon as possible. I don't want to leave any space for the Enemy to come in and mess with my family. Having peace in my house is so precious to me. A peaceful home is key to a happy marriage and happy kids.

Keep strife out of your marriage at all costs. True, we can't control what our husbands do, but we *can* control how we respond to it. No one can take us out of peace without our permission. Our emotions follow our thought life. As long as we keep control over our thoughts, we can keep control over our emotions.

For example, when you have a conflict with your husband, don't agree with the negative thoughts the Enemy tries to feed you. Don't agree with thoughts like *My husband doesn't appreciate me* or *My husband thinks I am a terrible wife* or *I can't stand my husband!* Cast those thoughts down. Don't allow negative thoughts to remain in your mind unchecked. If I allow thoughts like those to stay in my mind and meditate on them, I find myself getting angrier and even more offended. But if I check those thoughts and start thinking positive things about my husband, it is much easier to bring the conflict to a close. I start thinking the truth about my marriage instead. I intentionally bring to mind all the loving things my husband has done or said and what he really thinks about me. I remember all the reasons that I am thankful for him. It is not easy to go against the flow of negative thoughts, but it is imperative to not allow the Enemy to have his way in your marriage. The Enemy loves strife and offense and hates godly marriage.

Honoring Your Husband

It says in the Bible that a wife should honor her husband. So, what does "honoring" look like? It means that a wife respects her husband. Husbands need respect from their wives as much as wives need love from their husbands. As wives, we should not put our husbands down, emotionally or otherwise. We should not speak or act disrespectfully toward them at home or in public. Our homes should be a sanctuary that our husbands can look forward to coming back to. So, no matter what is going on in their lives, they know that they can always come home to a supportive, loving wife and a peaceful home.

I highly recommend reading the book, Love & Respect by Emerson Eggerichs. This book explains how wives need love, yet husbands need respect. It will truly be a huge help in having a happy marriage!

Your husband should be able to trust you completely. You should be his safe place. I have seen wives disrespect their husbands on social media, airing out issues within their marriages for all to see and judge. I bet if those husbands aired out their wives' dirty laundry on social media, they would not be happy about it at all, to say the least. Keep in mind that if in doubt, do unto others as you would have them do unto you (Luke 6:31). Not only is it disrespectful and dishonoring to broadcast private disagreements on the internet, it is also unjust. King Solomon himself said, in Proverbs 18:17, *"The first one to plead his cause seems right, Until his neighbor comes and examines him."* Have you noticed this to be true? The first one who complains seems right and just, until you hear the other side of the story. Therefore, when wives complain about their husbands on social media, it is unjust, because the husband's side of the story hasn't been heard. Not only that, those who read the outburst will normally side with the one who wrote it. Then, even after the disagreement is resolved between the spouses, these same people will continue to harbor offense against the husband. At the very least, he may no longer be esteemed in their eyes. This is the opposite of what the Bible says. We must look for ways to *honor* our husbands, not dishonor them.

How to Be a Satisfied Wife

We can also show our husbands that we honor them in how we fellowship or communicate with members of the opposite sex. If a potentially compromising situation arises, you need to ask yourself two simple questions: First, "Would I like it if my husband were doing this?" and second, "If my husband knew about this, would he approve?" If the answer to either question is no, then make sure you don't do it. For example, watch your thought life and make sure that you don't meditate on how handsome or how kind another man is. True, thoughts can sometimes cross our minds, and it's not a sin to notice that another man is attractive or kind, but we shouldn't meditate on it.

By meditate, I mean to keep it in the forefront of your mind and continue to think on it. It's important to keep your focus on your husband. Don't leave any room for the Enemy to cause you to be dissatisfied with your husband. Sometimes the thoughts that come are authored by the Enemy. I have heard this saying by Martin Luther: "You cannot keep birds from flying over your head, but you can keep them from building a nest in your hair."[1] This means that we can't always control what thoughts come into our minds. (Sometimes they are memories triggered by certain experiences or other related thoughts. At other times, the thoughts are suggestions from the Enemy to get us off track.) Therefore, we need to be vigilant about guarding our thought lives, casting down any thought that is ungodly or unprofitable.

In Matthew 5:28, Jesus said, *"But I say to you that whoever looks at a woman to lust for her has already committed adultery with her in his heart."* The same goes for a woman looking lustfully at a man. If we wouldn't want our husbands to think this way, we need to make sure that we don't think this way either. This is one reason that neither men nor women should watch pornography, either separately or together as a couple. Nothing good comes out of it. It will cause dissatisfaction in your marriage, as well as a laundry list of other issues. Besides, it is sin. God has much better for you. Delight in your husband and in your marriage bed. That is where the blessing is.

There are many other things that can influence us and bring dissatisfaction within our marriages. It is not just pornography that's the problem. Take romance novels, for example. These are not based on real life, and they can easily bring dissatisfaction within a marriage. Romantic movies may also cause dissatisfaction. There is no hard-and-fast rule about this, but use caution, and protect your heart and marriage at all costs.

Watching over Your Thought Life

Some women also become dissatisfied with their husbands through spending a lot of time on social media sites and the internet in general. They spend time looking at other men's toned bodies and Hollywood-type looks. The pictures may be photo-shopped and, for all they know, the men they are looking at may be self-centered and ungodly. (You can't judge a person based on their outward appearance.) Yet if we engage in this type of activity, it can cause us to lust after other men and, once again, become dissatisfied with the husbands that the Lord blessed us with.

Besides, the grass isn't greener on the other side of the fence. It is greener where you water it.

A harvest only comes when a farmer sows seeds. So, if you don't like the harvest that you are experiencing in your marriage, take a good look at the seeds that you are sowing in your marriage. Are you sowing selfishness and strife but expecting a peaceful, close-knit marriage? That makes about as much sense as a farmer sowing carrot seeds and expecting a harvest of strawberries. You can turn your marriage around by focusing on how you can be a blessing to your husband. If you're just focusing on yourself, what *you* want, and what *you* need, that is a recipe for misery. But when you serve your husband and become singularly focused on what you can do to be a blessing to *him,* then you will have joy. You will also notice that your husband's love tank will be full, and love will overflow back onto you. The Bible confirms this in Acts 20:35, which reads, *"It is more blessed to give than to receive."*

I knew a woman years ago who attended the same church that I did. She was married and having an adulterous relationship with another man. That man was also married, and he was committing adultery with this woman. Both of them left their spouses, believing that this new relationship would bring them the happiness they were searching for. They were married for a few years and had a child together. One day this woman said to me, "If I had known back then what I know now, I would never have left my first husband." She found out the hard way that the grass isn't greener on the other side.

If your husband was sent to you by God, then he is God's very best for you. You can have a full measure of joy and contentment in your marriage by guarding your heart, focusing on your husband, putting his needs above your own, and making sure that your relationship with Christ is first and foremost. Don't look to your husband to fill all the places in your heart that only Christ was meant to fill. No one can take the place of Jesus, so let your husband off that hook.

Not all married women look at other men on purpose, but some websites and apps are full of images like that. The problem is, where the mind goes, the man (or woman) follows. Every action that we have ever taken originated from a decision that we made, and that decision started off as a thought in our mind. Because of this, we need to stay vigilant over the thoughts in our minds. If we control our thoughts, we control our whole body. The action of adultery starts first as a thought in the mind that is not cast down. This is an important thing to remember. If you want to protect your marriage from dissatisfaction, discontentment, and strife, cast down any and all thoughts that aren't conducive to promoting oneness in your marriage.

If you have noticed that you have an issue in the area of your thought life, you alone have the power to change it. Simply repent and cast down any negative or sinful thoughts, and replace them with thoughts that are pleasing to God and pleasing to your husband. Act as if your husband is able to read your thoughts. If certain social networks or apps are a problem in your life, cut them off at the source. Protect your marriage and keep your eyes and heart pure before your husband and before God.

It is much more satisfying to live a holy and pure life and have a happy home than to fulfill the lusts of the flesh and cause the destruction of your marriage and family life. Fulfilling the lusts of the flesh *always* leads to destruction. You can be sure of that. Don't be deceived into believing otherwise. The Enemy would love nothing more than to destroy your godly marriage and home. Yet he only has that power if you let him. He needs your consent and cooperation to destroy your home and marriage. So, don't come into agreement with him by allowing his thoughts to stay in your mind and by choosing his stuff. Always cast down the thoughts he gives you. You can tell what they are because they don't line up with the Word of God. Protect and guard your marriage and home by always choosing God's thoughts and God's ways and by always following the peace of God in your heart.

The Deception of Social Media

Another stumbling block can be watching someone else's "perfect marriage" on Facebook. You can feel like your husband just doesn't measure up to *their* husband. Keep in mind that most people carefully choose what to post about their families on social media, and it may not be (and probably isn't) a balanced representation of what is really going on behind the scenes in their family. For instance, I am friends with a beautiful married woman who has lovely children, and every photo she posts shows a perfect, happy family. So, when I found out that she and her husband had been on the verge of divorce, I was stunned! It taught me that we cannot judge a family by what we see on social media.

With that being said, if a certain person is becoming a stumbling block in your life on social media, stop allowing yourself to view their posts. There are measures you can take to protect your eyes from that. Your marriage is precious. Do what you have to do to keep your marriage healthy, happy, and whole.

Interactions with Other Men

It is not just our thoughts, media, and social media that we need to be careful about. We also need to use wisdom regarding physical interactions with members of the opposite sex.

The rule of thumb is to always act like your husband is in the room, even in his absence. For example, a back massage from another man may seem innocent enough, but would you get a back rub from another man if your husband were right there with you? Another example would be allowing men to hug you, or even initiating hugs with other men. We always want to honor our husbands and make sure that we portray the truth to others that we are happily married and don't desire other men. When we hug other men, it can be misconstrued by them as interest. We want to make sure that we don't give off that impression in any way. This is how we honor our husbands. Likewise, we want them to show that same honor to us. A woman appreciates when her husband makes it very clear by his actions and words that he is off limits to any other woman but her.

A Godly Example

Another good example is Mike Pence, the current vice president of the United States. He has made it known that he will not dine alone with any woman other than his wife. He was being slammed by many people for taking that stance. However, this is godly wisdom. My husband and I follow this rule also. Not only that, we don't drive in a car alone with a member of the opposite sex unless we have a really good reason and have gotten permission from our spouse ahead of time. We also make sure that we are led by the peace of God. God sees potential pitfalls that we simply cannot see.

We don't want to leave any room for the Enemy, and we don't want our good to be evil spoken of. It is better to take measures like this to protect your marriage than to *not* have these boundaries and then find yourself in a compromising position. When my husband calls me to ask if it's okay if he drives a woman home from his workplace (which doesn't happen very often), it makes me feel really loved. I know that my husband loves and honors me enough to allow me to make that decision. I can't remember ever saying no, because my husband would never ask to drive a woman home who was attracted to him. It is always just something he wants to do to be a blessing and to help others out. But the fact that he asks me every time shows me that he holds me in high regard.

Be Careful Who You Confide In

Another example is using a member of the opposite sex as a confidant. When a woman pours out her feelings to another man and gets marital advice from him, it can cause a closeness between the two that should not be there. One of my friends once had a male friend that she would seek advice from. She found herself drawing emotionally closer to this man. She likened it to having an emotional affair. Her heart was moving in the direction of this man who was so kind to her and gave her advice. She realized what was happening and put a stop to it before any more damage was caused.

If you have a disagreement in your marriage that cannot be sorted out between the two of you, you need to each find a godly, seasoned, trustworthy man or woman from whom you can gain wisdom. (They must be people that you both agree upon.) Women need to only gain counsel from other godly women, and men from godly men, unless you are seeking counsel together and not separately.

On a different note, it is okay to have disagreements in front of your children, as long as the disagreements are civilized, which means no yelling, screaming, name-calling, etc. There should never be any of this in a marriage regardless, but especially not in front of the kids. This is damaging to them. You and your husband are the foundation of the family. If the kids perceive that the foundation is crumbling (even if it's not), it causes great distress to them.

However, having civilized disagreements and resolving them in front of the children is healthy. Children will see that having disagreements is a normal part of life. They will also see that disagreements can be sorted out in short order and that their parents still love each other regardless. This will set children up for success in their own marriages, because they will have a realistic idea of what a marriage is like.

Be a Blessing

Other ways that you can honor your husband include preparing meals that he likes, taking great care of the home and the children in his absence, and taking care of your appearance and health.

These are not hard-and-fast rules since not every mother is a stay-at-home mom; these are just examples.

My pastor recently shared that even though he loves ice cream and dislikes exercise, he only eats ice cream in moderation and exercises regularly to look good for his wife. As you see, it is a two-way street. Shouldn't we want to be a blessing to our spouses in whatever ways we can? I have always gotten back to pre-baby weight within a year after the births of my children. It hasn't been easy, but the Lord has always helped me and given me His grace to do it. I like looking good for my husband. I also like to feel good within myself. If I feel good about myself, it flows outward to the family.

As far as looking after the kids, cleaning the house, and preparing meals, these are things a wife can do to be a blessing to her husband. It brings me joy when I prepare a meal that my husband likes (and I like to hear the words of affirmation that follow). I also like to bless him by taking care of the kids well and by keeping a clean house (with the help of the kids) for him to come home to. My husband feels blessed by the sanctuary that I create and maintain in our home, and he blesses me by maintaining a good work ethic at work and by helping me around the home when I need it. He also likes to tell others about me and how I am such a blessing to him. This blesses me. I love to be a virtuous woman and to bring joy to my husband.

The Importance of Sex

This chapter wouldn't be complete without talking about sex. Before I got married, I didn't realize how important sex was in a marriage. But now I have the revelation! Husbands need passionate sex from their wives. Sex is one way that a husband shows his love to his wife. Also, the release that he gains from sex is a physiological need that he has. The Lord doesn't want us to be abused in the marriage, and your husband shouldn't want that either, but within the boundaries of a loving marriage, make sure that you make yourself available to your husband for sex. Also, make sure that you are passionate toward your husband during sex and not just wishing that it was over. Your husband needs you to be available in your body *and* your mind. This will be a huge blessing to him. Throughout the Bible, God makes it clear that the husband and wife relationship is a picture (a type or shadow) of Christ and the church. A very seasoned and godly instructor in my Bible college once said to our class, "Jesus and your husband want the same thing: that is, a responsive bride."

As we come together as husband and wife in unity during sex, it is spiritual warfare.

The devil doesn't care who you sleep with, as long as it's not your spouse. This is because sex, within the covenant of marriage, causes great damage to his kingdom.

I once read a story about a group of ladies who came together in a meeting and were complaining about their husbands. They were all talking about how they had asked their husbands to take care of jobs around the house many times and yet the jobs had remained undone. They all did not want to have sex with their husbands because they were getting frustrated by them. The leader of the meeting suggested a little experiment. She asked all the ladies to put their "honey-do" lists aside and just focus on loving their husbands and giving them what they needed instead. She asked them all to be a blessing to their husbands in the bedroom without any strings attached. The ladies all agreed and went home to make love to their husbands. When they all came back together for their next meeting, they all marveled at the changes in their husbands. It turns out that once their husbands' needs were met with intimacy in the bedroom, the husbands started working on their honey-do lists without being asked!

I don't mean that we should use sex as a means to manipulate our husbands to do what we want. But it just goes to show that once your husband feels valued by you making his needs in the bedroom a top priority, he will be so blessed that he will want to reciprocate and be a blessing to you also.

I have also heard that if you reject your husband's advances for sex four times in a row, it can really do damage to your marriage. Your husband will start emotionally drawing away from you. He wants to make love to *you*. He wants to be intimate with *you*. He wants to show you how passionate he is toward you. Unless you have a really good reason, don't turn down his advances. Better yet, *you* be the one to initiate. That will bless his socks off! Make him feel like he is your top priority by blessing him in this way.

Your Husband's Love Language

Also, make sure that you are speaking your husband's primary love language. If it is physical touch, make sure that you make it a priority to show him affection. If it's acts of service, make sure that you serve him in ways that he notices, and make him feel loved. If in doubt, ask him what sorts of things he likes you to do, and then do them. If his primary love language is words of affirmation, think of ways to compliment him and tell him you love him. If it is gifts, bring him something special from the store to let him know you were thinking about him while you were away. It doesn't have to be expensive. It's the thought behind it that counts. One time I brought my husband home his favorite candy. He felt so blessed by it because he knew I was thinking about him while I was absent from him. Lastly, if it is quality time, make sure that you give him uninterrupted one-on-one time. Listen intently to what he says, looking him in the eye.

Make sure your husband also knows what *your* primary love language is. Give him tips on what he can do to make you feel loved. Don't be afraid to make your needs clearly known. There is no use in not communicating your needs and desires and then getting offended because your husband cannot read your mind. Whenever I feel like I need to have my love tank filled, I don't hesitate to ask my husband for words of affirmation. I will even text him questions when we are apart, such as "How much do you love me?" "What do you love about me?" or "Can I please have some good words of affirmation?" He is always sweet to write back to me some loving words. Words aren't his strong suit, but he puts in the effort, and that means a lot. It shows me that I am his priority. And since he is mine, I try to be purposeful in filling his love tank by speaking his primary love language of physical touch. I try to give him back massages, hugs and kisses, etc. If I get busy and forget to do these things, he lets me know that he feels like he is my lowest priority. That is my sign that I need to get better at being affectionate toward him and not let my other responsibilities of the home and kids take precedence.

VII. Instructing Your Children

Earlier in the book, I revealed that there are three vital aspects to raising children well. They are correction, affection, and instruction. I have already covered correction and affection. I showed that correction is so important, but it cannot be administered effectively without the praise and affection your child needs. If you are withholding either affection or correction from your child, your child will grow up missing critical components that they need in order to develop into a secure, well-adjusted adult. Just as correction and affection are vital, so is instruction.

As I briefly mentioned earlier, we are all born as infants, and we learn everything as we go. If we are not taught how to do specific things in each area of our lives, we either need to figure those things out for ourselves, or go on with our lives lacking that information.

The information that our children need before they become adults is immense. For example, they need to learn how to walk, talk, groom themselves, multiply, divide, use the restroom by themselves, treat others with love, obey God, manage a household, etc. It is our duty as parents to equip our children with all the instruction they need while they remain in our care. We need to realize that although babies and children are small and cute, they are destined to become adults. One day they need to contribute to society through a solid work ethic and good moral character. They need to raise their own families, run their own households, do their own taxes and, most importantly, love and serve the Lord with all their heart.

We need to do our part to equip our children throughout their childhood and adolescence so that when it is time for them to move out on their own, they have a solid foundation. Therefore, it is important that we use childhood not only as a time of fun (which is necessary), but also as a time of equipping in preparation for adulthood. We all want our children to excel in life, to flourish in and outside the home. Therefore, it is vitally important to view our children as mini-adults and to regularly give them age-appropriate instruction and responsibilities to help them succeed as they move into adulthood.

Age-Appropriate Chores

When your children are young, it is very good to give them age-appropriate chores to do around the house. As they grow, you can increase the level of what they are required to do. As you release your child into a new level of responsibility, make sure you give them the necessary instruction on how to accomplish the task with excellence. For example, when it is time to fold the clean clothes, you can have your young child fold the small face towels and other simple items. Show them how it is done, and repeat as necessary. Praise them when they accomplish the task. Make sure that you don't give them too many items to begin with. You don't want to overwhelm them. Don't expect perfection. There is a season when you have to put aside your desire for everything to be folded perfectly. Guiding your children into new levels of proficiency and areas of responsibility is the priority.

Once your child has demonstrated a sound proficiency in the current task, take them to the next level and continue to build upon their knowledge from there.

Some parents feel bad when they put their children to work. They feel better about themselves when they are doing all the work themselves. This is detrimental to children. Even God gave Adam work to do in the Garden. It is healthy to work. We are designed to flourish when we are given a purpose and a goal to achieve. Idleness is the opposite of diligence, and diligence is a godly character trait that is important to instill within our children.

It is important to allow your children to have play time and time to just be kids. However, there must also be times when you give your children tasks to accomplish. This will give them a sense of achievement and contribution to the home, and it will also equip them to one day run their own households and lives with excellence.

I remember when I moved out of the house after I got married. There were some things that I could do very well, but there were a couple of things that I had no clue about. It was actually a bit embarrassing because my husband, who had been a US Marine for a while, had to teach me the things that I lacked. There were other things, like how to mother a newborn and raise my kids, that I just had to learn by trial and error and with lots of help from the

Holy Spirit. I did read books to help me, but they only proved to add to the difficulty of having a newborn. This is because I was trying to do everything perfectly, just like the book told me. But life is not always black and white, and babies do not all act the same way.

The best and most helpful advice that I received was from my mother and my older sister. They gave me wisdom and sound advice on how to take care of a newborn when I was a new mother. When you get advice from experienced mothers in your family, you know it's advice that has been tried and tested and works. You can put a greater level of trust on advice received in this way. The childrearing information that I received from experienced family members was extremely helpful to me. Because of this, I have realized how important it is for me to equip my kids in every area of life. I want them to be well-rounded individuals who can stand on the shoulders of what their father and I know and increase from there. Once they leave my care, I don't want them to have to spend time learning some of the basic things that I had to learn.

Managing Finances

Children should learn how to manage money, how to give, how to save, and how to pay bills. They should learn the importance of paying their bills on time and being good stewards of the money that the Lord has blessed them with. Some of us may not know very much about managing our own finances and may not feel equipped to teach our children how to handle wealth. Don't be discouraged by this. I am still learning how to be a good steward of the money God has blessed us with. Instead of running to the solutions of the world's system (for instance, going into debt), I'm learning to trust God to provide everything we need.

The good news is, there are many teachers in the body of Christ who have been given revelation on many topics, including how to manage finances God's way. All we have to do is seek them out and gain the knowledge we need about finances and other areas of our lives. Then we can teach our children to do the same. If we ask God, He will lead us to the teachers and the scriptures that have the answers we need. Matthew 7:7-8 says, *"Ask, and it will be given to you; seek, and you will find; knock, and it will be opened to you. For everyone who asks receives, and he who seeks finds, and to him who knocks it will be opened."*

As parents, we need to be constantly and diligently seeking the Lord for ourselves so that we are growing and gaining wisdom that we can pass to our children. Our children are worth it.

I could harp on this for a while, but you can see for yourself the wisdom of what I'm saying. It is vitally important to equip your children with instruction in every area of life. As you take care of the day-to-day, practical aspects of living, make mental notes that when your children reach a certain age, they will need to be taught to do certain things themselves. The Holy Spirit will reveal to you what to teach and when your children are ready for you to teach it. The Holy Spirit is your ever present help in time of need. He cares about your children and will be sure to help you do what He desires and requires you to do as a parent.

Cultivating Responsible Behavior

There is no such thing as adolescence in the Bible. People were considered either children or adults. When children are around fourteen years of age, it is important for you to begin to treat them as adults. Let them have more freedom to make mistakes so that they can learn from those mistakes. If we as parents constantly stand in the way of our adult children and their mistakes, they will never learn, and we will hinder their growth and their gaining of wisdom.

Recently my pastor told a story about a couple of college students. The two students were roommates in a dorm. It was the first time they had lived away from their parents. One of the students complained to my pastor that he was having a hard time waking up his roommate in the mornings. He would try multiple times each morning to wake up his roommate so he would not be late for class, but his roommate would just ignore him and would continue to sleep. My pastor gave him some sound advice. He told the boy that from that point on, he needed to get up as quietly as he could and leave for class without waking his roommate up. That way, the roommate would be completely responsible for his own life. If he chose to continue to act irresponsibly and sleep in, he would eventually feel the painful consequences of his own actions. He would have to make a decision about whether to continue to act that way or to make a change and begin to be responsible in that area.

My pastor also went on to explain that the roommate's mother was obviously one who constantly babied her son while he was still at home. She would act as his alarm clock and try to get him to wake up every morning, and he would continue to push the boundaries and wait until the last minute.

Do you see how coddling and babying our children as though they were still infants is not helping them, only hindering them? As parents, we need to give our growing children more and more responsibility and independence. We need to let them feel the negative consequences of their own bad choices. This is all a part of growing up. I know that it is not easy to watch our children make mistakes, but if we are truly interested in raising them to be wise adults, we need to use wisdom about when not to interfere with life lessons that they need to learn. If we constantly stand in the way of their negative consequences, we simultaneously stand in the way of their growth.

Another example is homework. You need to allow your teenage-adult to take responsibility for the completion of their own homework. It may be hard to stand back and watch your son's or daughter's negligence cause them negative consequences at school, but the experience that they gain through this will help them make the right choices in the future. However, constantly nagging them to get them to do the right thing will stand in the way of their consequences. This will only cause them to go around the same old mountain, so to speak, and they will not have the benefit of learning and growing from their mistakes.

Consequences

As children grow, be vigilant to listen to the Holy Spirit's leading, and give your children more and more responsibility, instruction, and freedom. You also may have to be the one to dish out the negative consequences. You may need to take away certain privileges around the home or outside the home until they learn to be responsible with the tasks you have given them.

For instance, if you ask one of your children to be responsible for a pet's daily water and food, and if your child does not do so of their own accord and without reminding, then you need to decide what consequence would be appropriate for your child (until they show consistency and responsibility in that area). Perhaps you might take away sweet treats, video games, or TV viewing. Your child would swiftly get the message that looking after the pet is a high priority. However, if you continue to remind your child over and over again about taking care of the pet, they will learn that there is no real consequence for shirking their responsibility. This will not equip them for the real world. This will only be a hindrance to their growth.

It is not easy to do this. It is very hard for me to take good things away from my children. I much prefer to bless them. However, I must do what is the best for the kids, and that means giving them consequences to help them grow in wisdom and understanding.

When my children were all really young, I baked a caramel birthday cake one day for one of my daughters. While I wasn't looking, my oldest son broke off a piece to sample it. When I asked him about it, he denied having done it. When the truth was finally revealed, I had to show him that his behavior and his lying were not acceptable. The next day was his sister's birthday party, and he wasn't allowed to eat any of the cake. This was hard for me to enforce because I wanted him to be blessed by eating the cake with us. However, this consequence bore great fruit. My son understood that what he did was wrong, and he never did it again. When the next birthday came around, he enjoyed cake with the rest of us.

Relationship with God

When we instruct our children, it is of vital importance that we instruct them about God and all that pertains to Him. Teach them how much God loves them and how He sent His only begotten Son, Jesus, to die for them so that they could have eternal life. Teach them what the Bible says. As God is showing you new revelations in life and in His Word, share it with your children too. Don't keep quiet about your relationship with God and all that He has done for you. Spend time with the Lord, read the Bible, and pray and worship in front of your children. Through your example, demonstrate what a normal Christian walk is meant to look like.

As I mentioned earlier, when I only had two children (and they were still babies), I loved the Lord, yet I wasn't spending time with Him and seeking Him like I should. I remember wondering, *How I am going to teach my kids about our loving God since there is no physical evidence of my relationship with Him?*

All that changed when I started to take my relationship with God more seriously. Now I live my Christian walk in full view of the children. I put on worship music and we worship together. They see me worship and dance, and they join me. They see me read and listen to the Bible, spend time with the Lord, etc. They will grow up knowing that these things are normal and will be more inclined to do likewise. I encourage my older children to spend their own time with the Lord. I encourage them to read the Bible for themselves and to listen to godly teaching. My oldest son especially likes to listen to podcasts of godly teaching. He listens to them when he goes to bed at night and likes to tell me in the morning what he learned.

It is important to teach your kids by example so that they grow up knowing that having a vibrant relationship with the Lord is normal. The children who grow up wanting nothing to do with the Lord are often children of parents who lived hypocritical Christian lives, professing Christ but living a life that was contrary. Because of this experience, those children wrongly deduce that there must not be a loving God. What a tragedy! The best thing you can do for your children's relationship with Christ is to have a vibrant one of your own to model in front of them. Part of modeling your relationship with the Lord includes loving and honoring your husband and respecting and loving your children.

What Not to Do

Some ministers of the Gospel have turned their children away from the Lord, not by being hypocrites, but by focusing on the Lord so much that they ignored their children. Instead of connecting with their children and spending quality time with them, giving them correction, affection, and instruction, they instead thought they were being holy by spending all their time ministering to others outside the family or by reading the Bible. These are good things to do, but not at the expense of your children. Jesus Himself made time to spend with children. Remember, children are mini-adults, and they need to grow up knowing that they are loved and cherished by their parents.

Here's another thing I do to help my kids develop their own trust relationship with the Lord: when the Lord answers prayer for me or my husband, I always share the praise report with the children. I want them to see for themselves that God is a good, loving Father who answers prayer. These are the two most important things you can teach your children: (1) God is a good God and (2) how to have a relationship with Him.

I cannot emphasize this enough! If your kids are constantly hearing about and witnessing the goodness of God and the power of God in *your* life, then they will grow up knowing, without a shadow of a doubt, that God is a good Father who answers the prayers of His children. You will set your children up for having a vibrant love relationship with the Lord for the rest of their lives. So, don't be silent about what the Lord is doing in your life. Magnify Him!

Cultivating Our Children's Gifts

Another key aspect of instructing our children is found in Proverbs 22:6, which reads, *"Train up a child in the way he should go, And when he is old he will not depart from it."*

The meaning of the phrase *"the way he should go"* is actually not referring to teaching the kids to have a relationship with Jesus, although this is an important thing. It is actually referring to training up your child according to his or her natural bent. A "natural bent" is a gifting that God has placed inside a person.

God creates us all with different talents and abilities. There are certain things that we are passionate about and have a gifting for that is unique to us. God wants us to find out the natural bent of each of our children and cultivate it. Ephesians 4:11 says, *"And He Himself gave some to be apostles, some prophets, some evangelists, and some pastors and teachers."* Notice that it says He gave "some," but what were all the rest? We are not all called to the fivefold ministry, yet we all have giftings given to us by our heavenly Father, and He wants us to use them for the edification of the whole body.

The gifting that He put in you is normally not hard to identify. It is your passion. Ask yourself what you would do for work even if you didn't get paid for it. Do you like to bake, create art, go fishing or hunting, take photographs, design new fashion, dance? Then this is your gifting. God wants us to identify the passion (or gifting) in our children and cultivate it. Since this is what they love to do the most, they will not depart from it. They will continue to grow and develop their gift and, in turn, be edifying to the whole body. We need each person operating in their individual giftings. If bakers didn't bake, fashion designers didn't create fashion, architects didn't create buildings, police officers didn't patrol the streets, we would all be missing out on partaking of their giftings and being blessed because of them.

A High School Friend

While I was in high school, I had a friend who was very talented in the area of fine art. We were sitting together one day at lunch, and she told me that she had recently met a little girl, around five years of age, who was passionate about art. The little girl had her whole life mapped out with what she was going to do with her art. My friend explained to me that she was impressed by the passion and focus this little girl had about art.

My friend subsequently shared the experience with her mother, who told her that my friend was exactly like that little girl when she was the same age. My friend was amazed! Thinking that it was wiser to pursue a more mainstream and "sensible" occupation, my friend realized that she had allowed her focus and passion for art to wane as she grew older. However, after this encounter with the little girl and the revelation she received from her mother, she decided that she would once again pursue her passion in art.

I have been amazed at the doors that the Lord has opened for my friend. She completed a fine arts degree at a prestigious university in Sydney, Australia. She has worked for art galleries, completed many art projects for clients, had her artwork displayed in galleries, and is now working as an art teacher at the same Christian high school we both attended. Once she made the decision to follow her passion, the Lord opened door after door for her. She is a living testimony of Proverbs 18:16: *"A man's gift makes room for him, And brings him before great men."*

My Niece

My niece is eleven years old at the time I'm writing this, and she has a real love for baking. Her mother (my sister) recognized this about her, so she went ahead and bought my niece baking tools and supplies so that she could help cultivate her passion. My niece has continued to flourish in her baking skills. She looks up recipes online, and her mother helps her buy the ingredients. She creates delicious cookies, cakes, and desserts. I am looking forward to seeing what doors the Lord opens for her as she continues to pursue her love of baking.

The Lord will reveal to you what giftings and talents He has placed inside your children. Ask Him, and He will make it clear to you. This is a vital part of raising happy kids. Once they know what God put inside them and are allowed to flourish in it, they will continue to develop their giftings, with joy and purpose, for the rest of their lives!

Healthy Habits

Another important part of raising kids is being a good steward over our children. We need to be diligent to steward their bodies so that they will be healthy. It is important that we teach them good hygiene, such as good bathing and showering practices. They need to learn to wash their hands regularly and wear clean clothing. We need to teach them about their bodies and how they will change as they start to go through puberty. In the right timing, as the Holy Spirit leads, teach them about sex. Let them hear how God intended sex to be, before they hear the world's perverted version of what God intended.

We also need to make an effort to feed our children as healthily as we can. They are not old enough to make wise decisions for themselves, so we need to make sure that we steward their bodies until they are old enough to take responsibility for their own choices.

When my children were young, I decided to allow them to drink mainly water. I was raised drinking very sweet drinks. Therefore, as an adult, it was hard for me to make the transition to drinking only water. I wanted to drink water as an adult for health reasons, and I wanted my children to grow up drinking water so that it would be easy for them to continue drinking it as an adult. I have noticed that my children love to drink water. I have given each of them their own drink bottle, and they drink water out of it every day. When their water gets low, they ask to have it filled up again. One time we were at a family function, and my mother-in-law was giving my kids some sweet juice to go along with their meals. My oldest daughter drank her glass, and when she was offered a refill, she asked for water instead. I was surprised. I would have never preferred water as a child. It showed me that I was doing the right thing. My kids are growing up enjoying and drinking a lot of water and will continue to do so as adults.

Another area that needs stewarding is our children's teeth. My parents never really stressed the importance of proper dental hygiene while I was growing up. As an adult, I am having to improve the way that I take care of my teeth since I now have many dental issues that need addressing. How I would love to turn back the hands of time and take care of my teeth properly from the beginning! I don't have that luxury, but I do have the responsibility of taking care of my children's teeth so that they won't have the dental issues that I'm having. It is not easy to do the proper daily brushing and flossing that is needed for so many children, but it is important. My dentist also told me that I need to limit the sweets or sugar that my children consume to help protect them against cavities. Because of this, I made a new rule: no sweets during the week. Sweets are only allowed on weekends. Of course, there is so much sugar in so many foods these days. Even so, I try to limit it during the week and have my children eat more fresh foods and less processed foods.

Dressing Modestly

Another way we steward our children's bodies is by how they dress and present themselves. We need to teach our children to dress modestly, as 1 Timothy 2:9 instructs. We are *in* the world, but we are not *of* the world. We need to teach our children to dress modestly to be a good representative of Christ in the earth. If we dress immodestly, like the world often does, people won't see a difference between the body of Christ and the world. Why, then, would they want what we've got if we're just like them? It's not just about the way we dress, but how we act and respond to situations. We need to shine as lights in this world to draw people to the Father. We can't do that and fit in with the world at the same time. James 4:4 states, *"Do you not know that friendship with the world is enmity with God? Whoever therefore wants to be a friend of the world makes himself an enemy of God."* Therefore, we need to teach our children how to dress to bring glory to God, not how to fit in with the world's immodest fashions (if the fashions are immodest).

Our Children's Reputation

We also need to be good stewards of our children's reputation. When our children are too young to be able to post online, parents are the ones who post about their children online. Some mothers tell all about the wrong things their children do and complain about their children on blogs and social media sites. This is unfair. We would be upset if someone portrayed us negatively online, so we need to be sure not to do that to our kids. Also, we need to be savvy to protect our children online. I lock down my Facebook so that no one can see any pictures of my children unless they are friends with me or my husband. I also don't "friend" anyone that I don't know. There are so many crafty and evil people online, and we need to make sure that we are not naive to the wiles of the Enemy. I once had a personal public Instagram account. I posted our family pics for all to see, until one day I had a wake-up call. A random young man in a different country started going through all my pics. In the space of about two hours, he "liked" almost all of them as he went through them. He would even take a break for about twenty minutes and then get back on my account and "like" some more. I was very concerned about it. Why would someone who didn't know our family spend *hours* looking at our family photos? I promptly set my account to "private." Our family's safety is so much more important than getting "likes" from strangers.

Education

Lastly, we need to be good stewards over our children's education and be diligent to help steward their learning. Invest in your children. Buy them books and help them read. Take them to the library and let them pick out books that interest them. Help foster in them a love for reading.

That being said, we need to make sure that we don't make education our god (or an idol in our hearts). Many people put so much emphasis on education that they have made it their god. Nothing should take the place of God in our lives. He should always be the focus.

There was a time when I felt a burden to make sure my kids excelled in their studies, since I was a homeschooling mom and was 100 percent responsible for their education. Then one day I miscarried a child (my third miscarriage), and the medical staff falsely believed that I had developed a tumor in my womb. They even sent me to a gynecologic oncologist. My husband and I had to stand on the Word and not give in to fear. This was a hard time in our lives, but when I was faced with the lie that I might die soon, it really put things into perspective for me. I realized that even though my children's education was important, it wasn't the main thing. So what if they were straight A students if they died outside of a relationship with Christ? In eternity, no one will care whether my child read fluently by the age of four.

So, I just want to take the pressure off you too, dear mama. Keep the main thing the main thing. Teach your children diligently as unto the Lord. But always remember that the most important thing we can teach them is that God is a loving Father and that Jesus died so they could have eternal life. The second most important thing we can teach them is to love others. If we raise passionate lovers of God and lovers of people, we are doing well. We want to bear fruit for eternity, so we always want to keep a heavenly perspective about all we do, and not get caught up stressing about things that won't matter in eternity.

VIII. The Family

The family is the nest for your children. It's the place where they are nurtured and where we create a culture of love through which they view the rest of the world. Through the love we show our children, we set them up for success in adulthood, helping them grow up secure and with a firm foundation. They know that they are loved by you no matter what, and they are also loved by their heavenly Father no matter what. They know that they can make mistakes and still be loved. You are a "safe harbor" for them to be completely honest with you, and they know that you will show them love and grace. Because your kids are firmly rooted and grounded in love, their love can, and will, flow out to others.

Have you ever heard the saying "Hurting people hurt people"? That is very true. The abused can become abusers (unless they receive healing from the Lord). While in school, I noticed that the kids who were bullies were the kids who came from broken or abusive homes, whether physical or emotional.

A High School Bully

I had a friend in high school who was verbally bullied by another girl. The two of them would engage in verbal sparring matches (which my friend would lose), and then my friend would spend a whole weekend trying to think of comebacks to say to the girl, only to be shot down again. The bully seemed to never be at a loss for words, and my friend just couldn't keep up. Later on in the school year, they settled their disagreement and became friends.

The girl who was the bully revealed the reason she was so good at arguing: it was because arguing was all she saw, heard, and experienced at home between her family members. I have heard this scenario more than once. The kids who are bullies and pick on other kids are the ones who are hurting, and it's because they are being picked on, abused, and/or neglected at home.

The kids at school who are promiscuous are often the kids who are insecure and looking for love in all the wrong places. We must be affectionate with our children and make sure that they feel loved. This will protect them from making the wrong choices when it comes to romantic relationships or relationships in general. When your children are secure and know that they are loved, they won't settle for second best. They can wait for the one spouse that the Lord has for them.

Respecting Parents

The kids who aren't taught to respect their parents are the ones who do not respect the teachers. This, in turn, causes problems for them in school. We need to teach our children to respect authority, as long as it doesn't violate the Word of God. When I was growing up, I was taught to respect my parents, so that carried over to my school life. I respected and obeyed the teachers and, in turn, I was always favored by them. This was a good thing because I was given opportunities that weren't given to more difficult students.

Motherhood and fatherhood are highly important callings in the kingdom of God. It takes deliberate effort and focus to raise a child well. To provide the best foundation for our children, we must think about our family life and look at the areas that need improvement. Happy families don't happen by accident. I read a quote that I thought was really in line with the whole gist of this book: "Children are not a distraction from more important work. They are the most important work."[2]

A Culture of Love

As parents, not only do we need to create a culture of love between us and our children, but we also need to create a culture of love between siblings. A lot of siblings grow up being mean to each other and speaking nastily to each other. They value their school friends more than they do each other. This seems to be the "norm." I used to think that way too. When I was a teenager, I remember going over my friend's house after school one day. I witnessed her treating her little brother so lovingly and kindly that I thought it was strange.

I have tried to foster close relationships between my children. Siblings are bound to have their disagreements with each other, but it is *how we handle* a disagreement that counts. With six children and their numerous daily interactions with each other, I have not always done this perfectly. However, I try my best to help my children reconcile with each other if a disagreement does arise. I help them to apologize to each other, and I encourage them to give each other hugs and tell each other, "I love you."

The other day, one of my young girls came to my room in tears, saying that her older brother didn't love her. She came to this conclusion because my oldest son gets frustrated with her at times because she doesn't always obey what he asks her to do. It broke my heart to see my daughter upset like that, so I spoke to my son in private. I shared with him what happened and that his sister didn't believe that he loved her. This upset my son, and he let me know how much he loves his sister. I asked him to go to her room and have a heart-to-heart conversation with her and make sure that she knew that he really did love her. He went and spoke to her privately in her room. A little later, my little girl came back to my room. This time she was all smiles. She shared with me what her brother had said and that she now knew he loved her. She also told me that she forgave him. I thought it was so sweet.

The Holy Spirit will give you insight and ideas for your own children as problems arise. You don't have to have it all figured out in advance. I sure don't.

Homeschooling Families

I have heard that homeschooling families have fewer problems with their children getting along with each other than families whose children go to school. This could be because the school separates children into different age groups, resulting in children having separate groups of friends. This could cause an older sibling to view a younger sibling as not equal to them. However, this doesn't have to be the case. Parents have a lot of say in the culture of their homes, and they can facilitate a love relationship between children from the beginning.

One thing I have never had to deal with is jealousy among siblings. I have heard many times that when new babies are introduced into a family, they are not well received by older siblings because of jealousy. I am not intimately acquainted with anyone else's family, so I couldn't honestly tell you what might lead to a reaction like that, but if your child feels secure in your love for them and knows that they are a valued member of the family, it would never leave room for jealousy.

Include older children in the plans you make for a new baby. Let them have a say in what you name the infant. Even if you don't intend to use the names they come up with, let your child know that you value their input. Help them get just as excited as you are about the baby's arrival. You might say, "You're going to be a great big brother (or sister)." Once the baby arrives, let them interact with the baby. Help them form a bond with them. Ask them to hand you the diapers and wipes, and praise them once they do. Thank them for being such a good big brother/sister. You might use different words, depending on the age of the child you're talking to. When your other children feel valued in this way, it won't leave any room for jealousy.

Godly Order

Some wives make their husbands sleep on the couch so that the children can sleep in their marriage bed instead.

Sometimes spouses focus on their children so much that their whole lives revolve around them. Their marriage suffers because of it and eventually falls apart altogether.

The best thing that you can do for your children is to foster a close and happy marriage first and foremost. And within that marriage, model healthy and godly roles and boundaries. The marriage came before the kids, and the marriage (and each spouse's relationship with Christ) is the firm foundation on which kids need to flourish. That is why your marriage needs to be a priority in your life. Take time out for each other. Think of ways to be a blessing to each other. Forgive quickly if offenses arise. Honor each other. Speak well of each other to others. Don't complain about your spouse to outsiders. If you need counsel, decide together who to speak to. It must be someone godly, so that they can provide godly counsel. Your husband must speak to a wise man, and you must speak to a wise woman. As I have mentioned before, it's important to not seek comfort from a person of the opposite gender. Leave no possibility of the Enemy getting a foothold in the marriage through emotional soul ties.

Parenting in Unity

Parenting should be done in unity. Do not correct each other's parenting in front of the children. Allow your children to see you as a unified front. If your husband tells the kids something they are not allowed to do or eat, make sure that you uphold and enforce what he has said, even in his absence. This will show the children that you honor your husband. It will also show them that what their father says carries weight and will be upheld at all times. Your actions will speak louder than your words. Your husband should also honor you in front of the children in the same way. If the two of you have a disagreement about a certain rule or punishment, talk about it later. Discuss it lovingly and out of the earshot of the children. Don't correct each other in front of the children.

Children learn so much more by watching your example than through anything you say. Let your life be a shining example for them to follow. We are not going to do everything perfectly while we are still in the flesh, but the Lord will give us the grace to do our best every day.

Submission

You have probably heard that the Bible says a wife must submit to her husband. In this day and age, a lot of people can't understand God's wisdom behind this, and all sorts of perversion has arisen surrounding it. What God meant by this was that wives should submit to their husband's protection, covering, and love. We are not meant to submit to their sin. No one should submit to sin.

When a husband loves God and seeks Him to find out His will for the family, and when he loves his family as Christ loves the church, it is easy to submit to him. I have a husband like that. I know that he uses wisdom and takes his role in the family seriously. He considers the welfare of his wife and children to be of paramount importance.

Also, God is a God of order. He made the husband to be the head of the home. It doesn't mean that he is better or more important than his wife. It means that the Lord gave him this role to establish an order in the home. He is the first of equals. As wives, we know that the husband should have the last say in matters of the home. And ultimately, husbands are accountable to God for how they steward the families they were entrusted with.

I have noticed that the Lord will often reveal to my husband the next step our family needs to take. My husband will share with me what he believes the Lord is saying and will ask for my input. I have found that it is normally not anything I have been thinking, and I may even be opposed to the idea at first. But within a few days, the Lord starts putting that same desire in my heart, and I come into agreement with my husband.

For instance, early in our marriage, we were living in Australia. I was so happy to be there with my husband because I am an Australian citizen and he is an American citizen. It was nice to have him in my hometown. However, my husband started talking to me about moving back to the USA. He felt like the Lord was leading us to do that. At first, I was adamantly opposed to the idea. I was happy where I was. However, after a few days, the Lord started working on my heart. I started losing my desire to be in Australia and started getting excited to move. My husband didn't have to force his will upon me; he didn't even try. He knew that if this was the Lord leading us, I would eventually come into agreement. And that's what happened.

I have learned over time that I can trust my husband's leading. I know that he is not given to whims when it comes to his family. He seeks the Lord and knows that not only does God give him direction for his family, but there is also perfect timing. I am not saying that he has never made a wrong move. We all grow in the Lord and gain wisdom as we go, but my husband leads me with the wisdom he has at the time and with lovingkindness. It is not hard at all to submit to him and follow his leading.

Future Spouses

This is why it is so important to marry the right person to begin with. We should talk to our kids about their future spouses so that they have it ingrained in them that they can trust God to lead them to the person that He has for them. When our kids are at the right age, we should also let them know the importance of sexual purity and saving themselves for their future spouses.

Our pastor was a youth minister years ago. He had all the young women and young men under his care write letters to their future spouses about how they were going to save themselves for them (emotionally and sexually) as a gift to them. Then he had them keep the letters in their Bibles. The idea was to eventually be able to give the letter to their spouse with their promise fulfilled.

He shared the testimony of a young girl who wrote the letter and sealed it up so it could not be prematurely read. She kept it between the Old and New Testaments in her Bible. Years went by, and she got married to a man of God. She opened that letter and read it to him on their wedding day. She contacted her youth pastor and shared with him how profoundly that simple act of letter writing had impacted her life. It wasn't that writing the letter had any power in itself; the letter just helped the young woman realize how important it would be to her future husband that she save herself for marriage, and it helped her keep her promise.

Although it is limiting God by saying that God has *just one person* in mind for everyone, God does have a particular person that He will lead us to at any one time in our lives. However, if we 'blow it' for whatever reason and don't come into agreement with God's leading, that doesn't mean that God can't lead us into another blessed union. As Andrew Wommack correctly states, "God is at least as good as a GPS (Global Positioning System). When you are driving and take a wrong turn, the GPS doesn't say, "Too bad! You blew it! You'll never get to your destination now!" No, it says, "Recalculating..."" So, God has someone in mind for everyone at every point in their lives, but He also gives us free will. It is imperative that we teach our children to follow God's leading in choosing a husband/wife. Only God sees the heart of an individual.

The only stipulation found in the Bible about choosing a future spouse is that the potential spouse *must* be a fellow believer in Christ. That's it. So, this is something we want to be careful to heed and teach our children to heed also. Other than that, the wise thing to do is to take baby-steps in moving forward into a relationship that may lead to marriage. Teach your children to partake in lengthy conversation with this person, making sure that there are no 'red flags' that arise in their spirits about anything concerning the other person. It is also biblical wisdom to seek wise counsel with other mature believers about the relationship. The Bible states that in a multitude of counsellors there is safety. These are all practical and wise things that we can instill into our children while they are still young, to set them up for success in choosing a husband or wife. This will give them a solid foundation on which to build a life, and raise godly, happy children upon.

God knows everything about everyone and also knows everything about the future. He is the only one who can be trusted to pick out our future spouse. I think about my ex-boyfriend, for example. He wasn't even a Christian when we were dating. I didn't get along with his family very well. I don't think they liked me very much. I am so glad that

I yielded to God when I did and trusted Him to choose my husband for me. I know that I wouldn't have grown in my relationship with Him as much as I have. I wouldn't have such a godly, selfless husband, and I wouldn't have moved to the USA and graduated from Bible college. The list goes on and on. Not only that, I get along with my husband's family very well. They all love me. Everything has been blessed from the beginning. The blessing of God has been evident on our lives from the beginning. I am more and more convinced every day that I married the right person.

My Personal Love Story

Let me share with you how I came to allow the Lord to pick out my husband. I was dating my ex, and I wasn't happy. I felt like I had a ball and chain around my ankle, and I was always trying to get my boyfriend to come up higher in the things of God. My pastor at the time shared with me what he could see me with a dynamic Christian, someone who loved the Lord so much that we would just mesh together like the gears on a clock as they turn. My heart yearned for that. To make a long story short, I broke up with my ex, even though it caused me physical pain in my stomach. I knew I was doing the right thing. Shortly thereafter, the Lord made sure I was in the right place at the right time to meet my husband. I want to share my love story with you to show you what God can do when you yield to Him.

Here is the story:

My phone beeped with a text message. I walked over to my bedside table and checked my phone. The message was from my friend Maggie. She asked if I wanted to go into

Sydney city with her while she attended a birthday party for a friend. (I lived about thirty minutes outside of Sydney, Australia, at the time. I was raised in Australia after my family emigrated from Germany, where I was born.) My first reaction was to decline. I was a homebody. I rarely went out. I was most comfortable and happy in my home around my family. I laid the phone back down on the bedside table and started to walk out of my bedroom, leaving the text unanswered. As I walked out of my room, a question popped into my head and stopped me in my tracks. It was the Lord (even though I didn't believe I could hear His voice back then). He said very clearly, "Why don't you go?" It was succinct enough to stop me from walking out of my bedroom. I thought to myself, *Well, why don't I go? I am twenty-one. It's a Friday night. Everyone else my age will go out. Hmm . . . I guess I will.*

I replied to Maggie, and later that night I drove her car into the city. When we reached the inner city on our way to Darling Harbour, we stopped at a traffic light. I noticed a group of about four marines in camouflage uniform crossing the road in front of us. They each had shopping bags in their hands. Somehow, I knew that they were American. It sparked my interest because I had spent my life trying to join the Royal Australian Air Force as a fighter pilot, and I was interested in the military.

Maggie and I parked and headed to Pontoon Bar on Darling Harbour. We walked inside and joined her group of friends. (Will later told me that he saw me walk in. He said that I caught his attention right away and that the Holy Spirit highlighted me among all the ladies who were there that night. He thought that there was something special about me. He also noticed that I was dressed more modestly than all the other women.)

Meeting My Husband

I sat with Maggie's friends and grabbed a bite to eat (since I didn't drink). After a while, Maggie, her friends, and I decided to go to the other side of Pontoon and dance on the dance floor. We were dancing in a circle (as girls often do) when I noticed an African American man come over and try to squeeze in our circle right next to me. He made me uncomfortable. To break the ice, I asked him, "Are you American?" He replied, "Yeah! How'd you know?" I told him that I was just a good guesser. (The truth is, it was an educated guess. Australia is a really multicultural country, but it's rare to see African Americans there.)

After about two minutes, Maggie wanted to leave the dance floor, and I decided to leave with her. I told the man that it was nice to meet him. He said that his name was Will. I told him my name was Dana. (I was debating about whether it was a good idea to give him my name.) We shook hands and I left.

Back on the other side of Pontoon, another marine started up a conversation with me. I was very unimpressed by his topics of conversation, and I wanted to get away from him. I did the girly thing and grabbed Maggie and headed to the restroom. On the way to the restroom, we had to squeeze down a narrow path beside the dance floor. It had people lining it. When we almost reached the restroom, Will all of a sudden stood before me. He said with a smile on his face, "Hey! You came back!" I replied awkwardly, "Yeah, I came back." I let him know that if he wanted to talk, I would be back in a minute and he could follow me back to our seats. He waited and walked over with me. As we chatted, I was very impressed by him. I thought he was very sweet. I remember very clearly one thing he said: "I just want to find a wife and raise my kids in church." I said to him, "You are going to make someone very happy one day." (I didn't know at the time that it would be me!)

My Focus on the Lord

You see, I was done with dating the wrong person. The next man I started a relationship with was going to be my husband, and I was waiting for the Lord to show me who he was. I didn't think it was Will, because he was American and only in Sydney for a few days. Will was a US Marine and had just come back from fighting in the Iraq War. He was one of the first people to cross the border from Kuwait into Iraq, and he helped pave the way to Baghdad. Traveling on the USS *Pearl Harbor*, he was heading back to California via Sydney, Tonga, and Hawaii.

The night progressed, and Maggie needed to go home. I gave Will my phone number and email address and told him that it was nice meeting him. Then I headed home with Maggie. It was Friday, June 20, 2003.

I received a call from Will a couple of days later, and he invited me out to lunch. My sister Jaci and I caught a train into the city and met up with him and another marine. (Marines are required to travel in pairs for security and accountability. It is called the battle buddy system.)

Will and I ate lunch, and Will paid for me. I liked that because I had been on dates where I'd had to pay. Will proved that he was a gentleman. We ate and talked. Then he bought me some vanilla fudge (my favorite!). We sat in the sun for a while and then went to get some coffee. Will wanted to buy me something at the café we went to, but because I didn't want him to have to pay again, I told him that I didn't want anything. He was/is such a gentleman.

We talked some more, and I grew more and more impressed with him and with his relationship with the Lord. I would've stayed and talked for longer, but Jaci wanted to get back home. I tried to make her stay, but she wouldn't listen. So, I had to leave too. Will walked us to the train station. And before I had even arrived home, he called my parents to make sure that I arrived safely. When I did get home, Will and I talked on the phone some more. I remember him saying, in his American accent, "I think you're a perfect angel." Aww. (I hope I don't embarrass him by saying that.)

I didn't see Will again before he left on the ship. We emailed back and forth until he got to Hawaii. Then he called me again, and we talked for hours. We emailed again as he sailed for California. I remember that it was the Fourth of July. Because of the time difference, Will had the Fourth of July twice on ship. Once back in California, Will called me pretty much every day. He would call me when he got home from work. He would talk to me sometimes all night long (using up an eight-hour international calling card) and then realize it was time to get up and go to physical training and morning formation. Oops! We spoke for hours and hours each day.

Eventually we realized that we had a lot in common and wanted the same things out of life. I got to speak to his family, who were really welcoming to me right from the beginning. Will and I started to talk about marriage. He bought a wedding ring and invited me to America to be his date for the Marine Corps birthday ball in Las Vegas, Nevada. I wanted to be his date, so he purchased me a ticket for November 6. Will called my dad and nervously asked for my hand in marriage. My dad gave it to him. (My parents had been really supportive of our budding relationship.)

Being Bold as a Lion

I flew out of Sydney Airport for my first flight to America. I was really concerned the whole way there. I prayed, *Lord, please help me to recognize him when I get to the airport.* Haha. I had only seen him those two short times in Sydney and only in a few photos since then, so it was a legitimate concern.

Thirteen hours later, I arrived in LAX. After I got my luggage, I walked into the arrivals lounge. All my fears dissipated, as the first person I saw was Will. He was in front of everybody, looking at me with a huge grin on his face. He greeted me and kissed me. He smelled so nice. Apparently, he had been driving the airport workers nuts, asking them over and over, "When is the plane going to land?" and "Why hasn't it landed already?" He ended up introducing me to one of them.

Will found a payphone and called my parents to let them know I arrived safely. I hadn't even thought about doing that. He was so responsible and protective.

As we were driving to Oceanside, California (right outside the marine base), Will watched the road, and I watched him. I remember looking at his ears and thinking, *He's got perfect ears.* I know I must've made him uncomfortable.

So, we explored the military base and saw some of California, just spending time with each other. We were really happy. A lot of his marine buddies didn't think I was real. They thought Will had gotten my picture off the internet and was just lying about me. Some of them said, "Oh, you're real!" Will was grinning from ear to ear.

One evening a few days later, Will took me on a long walk on a beach at sunset. He told me what I meant to him. It was so sweet. He got silent because he was holding back tears. Then he asked me to marry him. I obviously said yes.

Las Vegas!

A few days later we headed to Las Vegas for the birthday ball. We booked into a hotel room and got dressed up for the ball. It was a great experience. Will was so sweet. Every time I had to go to the restroom, he escorted me there and waited outside just to escort me back to the table. I want my sons to be just like their daddy!

After the ball, we tried to find a chapel to get married in. There were a lot. We found an Elvis one and even the drive-through one. It was so late, and it had already ticked over into the next morning. We decided to go and get some rest and try again the next day. The next day we found Little Chapel of the Flowers. We booked in for around 4 p.m. that afternoon and went to freshen up. When the time came, we only had Will's friend and his girlfriend to be our guests. It was a quick ceremony. Under ten minutes and we were married!

Photos were taken, and we got in the car and headed back to Oceanside. While we were on the way, we called Will's parents to let them know we were married. Will handed the phone over to me, and I listened as his father prayed a blessing over our marriage. It meant a lot to us.

At that point, I had seen Will twice in Sydney for a

few hours. I had arrived in the US on November 6 and got married on November 11. So, that added up to less than a week of face-to-face time altogether. If my trust hadn't been in the Lord, I wouldn't have been so bold.

When we got back to Oceanside and into our hotel room, we called my parents to let them know that they had a new son-in-law. They were so happy. They went out to get chips and chocolate so that they could celebrate. I thought that was cute.

After two weeks were up, I had to get back to Australia and wait for Will to get a house on base before I could come back and live with him. I was so sad to leave him. I remember sitting on the plane, looking back over the lights of Los Angeles as I flew away from my husband. A few hours later I heard a song that reminded me of all the fun times we had just had together, and I cried! I called Will from the airplane. He was happy to hear from me. Apparently, he had just spent two hours talking to my dad because he was missing me. Aww.

Reunited at Last!

In January, Will received housing on base. I was able to fly back to finally be a wife to my husband. It was not easy to be in a new country and to be the wife of a military man who had to be away a lot for training to get ready to go back to the war.

The Lord blessed us with our first daughter almost right away. Everything was new. Will was sent back to Iraq when I was six months pregnant, and I went back to Australia to give birth. Four months after our daughter was born, I flew back to the US and waited for Will to get back from the war. Then I introduced him to his new daughter.

As you can see, the Lord had His hand in everything that happened. My husband and I couldn't have fabricated it if we had tried. We grew up on opposite sides of the world and were from two different cultures, yet the Lord had us meet on an appointed day and hour. It was amazing to me how much we had in common.

I can't imagine how different my life would be if I hadn't obeyed the leading of the Lord and gone into the city with my friend that night. I had no idea that my whole life was going to change. I have now lived in the USA for over a decade in all. My husband and I have been married for over fourteen years as of this writing, and we have six beautiful children together. We are still so happy and more in love than ever. It's not that we haven't had any issues or challenges, but with Christ at the center of our marriage, He always brings us through victoriously.

Yielding to God

As you can see, when I gave up trying to make things work myself, the Lord showed Himself strong in my situation. He made sure I was in the right place at the right time to meet the husband He had for me. I could never have organized that on my own.

I wasn't the only one who yielded to God. My husband also came to the end of himself right before we met. He was raised in a Christian home. He loved the Lord, but he wasn't living a completely holy life after he joined the marines. While he was deployed to Iraq, he saw how quickly and easily a person's life can get taken away. He realized that he needed to stop doing his own thing and needed to get serious again about his walk with the Lord. When his deployment ended, he was sitting on the ship on the way to Australia and started talking to the Lord. Since the age of sixteen, my husband had always had a heart to be married. He had searched for a wife in his own strength, but not one of the relationships worked out. So, while he was talking to the Lord on the ship, he told Him, "Lord, if I never get married, I am all Yours." Little did he know, he was only twenty-four hours away from meeting me, his future wife. God is so good! He only needs a yielded heart that trusts Him.

The Order of the Home

God is the first priority in the marriage relationship. I have no idea how anyone stays married without Him. Whenever anything goes awry in my marriage, I am quick to ask God to help me and to help fix the problem. God has the answer for everything. Oftentimes the answer is to forgive or to humble yourself and ask for forgiveness. God will never give you advice that goes against His Word. That's why it is good to read the Bible to find out what God says. I like to listen to an audio Bible while I am getting ready in the morning. It is a good way to get the Word of God when you are a homeschooling mother of six kids! (You gotta do what you gotta do, right?) While I am getting ready and listening to the Word, I simultaneously pray in tongues. I also try to spend time with God throughout the day by putting on worship music, hearing His voice and writing down what I hear, etc. It is little disciplines like these that keep my relationship with God as the number one priority. Likewise, my husband spends his alone time with the Lord whenever he can. When we are each solid in our own relationship with Christ and complete in Him, our marriage is healthy and blessed. We don't try to make one another fill the void that can only be filled by God Himself. Trying to get fulfillment from your spouse and being needy will only lead to burnout. God is the only one who can fill every need and desire of your heart. So, look to Him instead.

After your relationship with God, your relationship with your spouse is the next most important relationship. Your husband was there before the kids were, and he will still be there once the kids have left the nest. Don't get me wrong. The kids' needs are important, but your spouse needs to be your priority. I have heard of couples who grew apart once their kids arrived because they devoted all their time and energy to their children. Once the kids moved out, the couple ended up separating because the kids were the ones holding the marriage together. This is sad. Make each other a priority for your sake and for the sake of your kids.

As I previously mentioned, some mothers sleep in the marriage bed with their children and make their husbands sleep on the couch for years on end. I would bet that their sex lives are also nonexistent. This is out of order. It is called a marriage bed for a reason. It is for you and your husband. I'm not saying that your kids can't sleep in your bed on occasion, but this should not be the norm. When my babies were very young, I had them in the bed with Will and me. But it wasn't long before they were sleeping in their own beds and staying there.

After God and your husband, the next priority is your children. Make sure that your friends and your job don't come before your kids. Sure, it is important to make a living, but if at all possible, your husband should choose a job/career that will allow him quality and quantity time with the children. And if it's possible for you to be a stay-at-home mom, that's your family's best option. It will allow you to have the most godly influence on your children. My husband and I desired from the beginning that I stay home with the kids, and God has always honored that and blessed us so that I could. Except for working part-time as a prayer minister for Andrew Wommack Ministries for a few months, I have not been employed since Will and I have been married. I took that employment while I was earning a degree in biblical studies at Charis Bible College. I believe that the Lord wanted me to do that job for a short season so I could have the ministry experience and be a blessing to His people. While I was working, Will spent time with the kids instead. One of us was always with them.

My Father's Sacrifice

I didn't realize it when I was a kid, but when I became an adult, my father told me that while my siblings and I were young, he had an opportunity to use his hard-earned and expensive commercial pilot's license to be a pilot in rural Australia. However, although he would've loved to have had that job and the income and prestige that went along with it, he instead decided to start his own business as a brick cleaner. He didn't particularly like the job, and he definitely didn't prefer it over being a pilot. But he chose it so that he could spend time with his five kids every morning before we went to school, and be home at a reasonable hour. And because he was his own boss, he could also take days off when he wanted to. Like I said, I didn't realize his sacrifice for us at the time, but I truly appreciate it now. I have very fond memories of spending time with my dad when I was growing up. I know that his decision had a great deal to do with how secure I am today as an adult, wife, and mother.

I think it's sad that little ones get dropped off at daycare at the break of dawn and then don't get picked up by their parents until nighttime. I know that some parents don't have a choice, but believe God for better. God wants *you*, not a childcare worker, to raise your children. Believe Him for a better job or better circumstance. God will answer your prayers and give you the desire of your heart. I have seen him make a way where there was no way.

I have a friend who works for an insurance agency. She believed that the Lord wanted her to go to Charis Bible College. The problem was, her job and home were about a four-hour round trip from the college. She decided to trust God, and without a safety net, she told her employer that she would be leaving in a few months to attend Bible school. After a short period of time, her employer asked her whether, rather than leave altogether, she would consider doing the same job, but working from home. She was thrilled. She was able to work from her daughter's home, which is only a short drive from the school. The Lord worked it out so that she was able to attend Bible college *and* keep her job.

God is so good. Our God is not a respecter of persons. If He can make a way for my friend, He can, and will, make a way for you too! Just believe that He will, and be obedient to what the Holy Spirit is telling you, even if it doesn't make sense to your mind. God always knows better, and you can always trust Him.

Children Are the Priority

I once read about a powerful, well-renowned minister of God who moved in signs, wonders, and miracles.

Dana Bellamy

This man had kids too, but instead of keeping his kids as a priority, he spent every minute focusing on spiritual things. He was always meditating on the Word of God and focusing on the things of God. He could be in the same room as his kids, but he was never available to them. Because of this, his kids grew bitter, and they turned away from their relationship with their father and the Lord. The minister's marriage ended also. How tragic.

This minister realized what he had done was wrong, but it was too late. He ended up getting married again and having more children. But this time he was a good father, spending a lot of quality and quantity time with his kids. This time his kids ended up growing up joyful and loving the Lord. They were not bitter toward God or their father in any way.

This true story impacted me greatly when I read it. It showed me that how I raise my kids will seriously affect their relationship with Christ. It also showed me that I need to be available to my children and not neglect them for the sake of the ministry. Jesus even demonstrated how important children are in Mark 10:13-16, where He rebuked the disciples for not allowing the children to come to Him. He also took time to take the children up in His arms and bless them. Jesus is our perfect example for ministry. If He placed an importance on children, we need to also.

Ministry should never come before our families. Ministry is good, but only once our husband's and children's needs are met. There have been times when friends have called me during the day, needing ministry or help in one way or another. Yet if I am busy with my children, I've asked them to call back at a more opportune time. Although my heart is to help, I have to set boundaries in place to protect my family time and to show my children that they are my

150

priority.

Beware of Overcommitting

Another thing to watch out for is making commitments to do things that will encroach on your priorities, which are your husband and children. It is so easy to say yes to people when they ask you to do things for them. However, you must first make sure that it won't take precious time away from your family life. For instance, when I went to Bible college at night, I was asked to sing with the night school worship team one night as they were practicing. I thought it would be fun, so I said yes. The team was impressed by my voice and asked why I hadn't joined them to lead worship at night school. I let them know that although I would have liked to do that, all the practice time required would take time away from my more important roles of being a wife and mother.

I always try to be mindful about not putting too much on my plate. It is not virtuous to be busy. I try to keep the main thing the main thing, and if I am in doubt, I follow the peace of God.

My pastor once shared how he learned to keep his wife and children a priority in the demanding role of being a pastor. He realized that if he allowed people to call him at all hours of the day and night, his family life and relationship with his wife and kids would suffer. He also told a story about another pastor who was walking out the door to leave on a much-needed vacation with his wife and kids. As he was leaving, he heard the phone ring. His family begged him not to answer it, but he did anyway. The person on the other end of the phone explained that they had just had a death in the family, and they needed him to come and minister to the family. So, he chose to stay and put ministry in front of family. This pastor needed to put boundaries in place so that his family time was kept as a high priority.

My pastor shares the ministry responsibility with two other people. They are each on call for one week out of three. That way, they each have two weeks of quiet, predictable time with their families. Another thing my pastor does is to put his family time in the schedule. That way, he won't be tempted to schedule something else in its place. He just tells people, "Sorry, I am completely booked out that day." This sends a message to his family that they are the top priority in his life. His kids grew up loving the Lord and having a great relationship with their parents.

So, to recap, the order of priority in the home is God, your husband, your kids, and then work and ministry. If you set proper boundaries to keep everyone in their proper place, you will have a marriage and family life that flourishes and is blessed. You will also have a vibrant relationship with Christ and healthy boundaries for work and ministry.

IX. The Grace of God

Let us therefore come boldly unto the throne
of grace, that we may obtain mercy, and
find grace to help in time of need.

Hebrews 4:16, *KJV*

It was Mother's Day, and the youngest of my five kids
I had at the time, was not even a year old. It was meant to be
a happy day, yet the day was so stressful and difficult that I
ended up in tears. I had no idea what was wrong. Normally,
I could take care of my children easily without any dramas.
Every day just flowed with ease. But for some reason, this
day was different. This day was very difficult.

As I cried and poured out my heart to my husband,
he reminded me that I had God's grace to look after my
children well and that I was never doing it on my own. He
also pointed out that when I relied on God for His grace,
everything just flowed effortlessly for me as a mother, so
much so that many who saw our family commented that I
was just a "natural mother" or even a "supermom." (Yet this
was not true. Mothering hadn't come naturally for me at all.

I had to learn everything as I went along.)

So, what was the problem? The Holy Spirit quickened to me a conversation that I'd had with my husband just the day before. Even though we had five children at the time, from eight years old all the way down to an infant, we were talking about possibly trying for a sixth child. The thought of adding another infant to my already large crew was overwhelming. It was stressing me out. You see, I had taken God out of the picture and had seen myself doing it alone—as if God had ever left me to do it alone! That was foolish thinking.

During our conversation, my husband and I had decided to stop at the current five kids that we had. (We obviously changed our minds later.) The decision to stop at five kids gave me a flood of relief, and I said to myself, *Phew! I can easily handle the five I already have.* Yet the very next day was the hardest day ever! I realized that I had unknowingly moved myself out of the grace of God that I was effortlessly operating in, and I was trying to mother my children through the flesh. In other words, I was trying to do it on my own and in my own strength and ability. Galatians 3:3 comes to mind: *"Are you so foolish? Having begun in the Spirit, are you now being made perfect by the flesh?"*

When I realized my mistake, I repented to the Lord and again started relying on Him to give me the grace to flow in my role as a mother. The change was immediate. This was the first time I really realized how much I relied on God's grace every day. It wasn't until I operated outside of it that I realized how much of my success as a mother was due to the flowing of the Holy Spirit through me. It has been years since that time, and I have never been so foolish again to think that I could do any of this without the daily grace of God.

A Minister's Example

One time I heard a story about how powerful the grace of God is. A minister was known to move powerfully in the Spirit as he flowed musically on the piano, singing songs that he created on the spot. The music was wonderful, and the songs rhymed and flowed effortlessly. One day the minister asked the Lord, "Lord, how much of this is me, and how much is You?" That night the minister went onto the stage like he normally did, preparing to minister on the piano and sing. He became very perplexed because, as he looked at the keys on the piano, they looked foreign to him. He had no idea how to even play the piano anymore. As he tried to think of a song to sing, nothing came to him. He could not think of one rhyming word. Humbled by the experience, he realized, "It is all You, God!" He repented and came back under the grace and anointing of God, and everything flowed out of him as before.

That is exactly how I felt that Mother's Day. I have never forgotten that day, and I ask the Lord for His grace every morning.

As a matter of fact, this morning I took all six kids, ages twelve down to four months, to the dentist without my husband. Three of the little ones were getting routine checkups and cleanings. The night before, I had started feeling a bit stressed about what I would have to do the next day. However, when I woke up this morning, I asked the Lord for His grace, and I trusted Him to be with me all day and to make everything flow effortlessly.

I ended up being in the dental office for two hours. I had three children occupying two different dental rooms at different times, plus I always had a bunch of my kids in the waiting area, including my four-month-old baby. But praise

God, everything went smoothly. The kids had a great time at their dental appointments, and the baby slept the entire two hours! The dental staff even commented on how well behaved my kids were. God is so good.

Increased Grace

What God calls you to do, He equips you to do. So, as the Lord gives you the desire of your heart and blesses you with more children, He will also increase the amount of grace that is available for you to operate in. There will always be more than enough grace. We just need to be sure that we don't have the mindset of "Okay, God. I've got this." We will only be successful in raising happy kids if we stop trying to do it in the flesh and in our own strength, and instead rely solely on His grace to flow through us.

As I mentioned earlier, when I became a mother for the first time, I wasn't prepared at all. Yet the Holy Spirit has taken me by the hand and taught me what to do by giving me thoughts or ideas, or He has led me to the information I needed. Sometimes He does that through a book, article, or YouTube video, or He will even send me people to give me timely advice. God is faithful. If you are teachable and rely on Him to help you, He will come through for you.

Not only will the Holy Spirit give you information, but He will also bring that information back to your remembrance when you need it. You are never alone.

No matter how many kids you have or what their ages are, God will equip you with the grace you need to flow effortlessly in your daily mothering. It will come with ease. All you have to do is ask Him for it and receive it as the

Scripture says. Every morning I pray a simple prayer: "Heavenly Father, I ask You for and receive Your grace for this day. In Jesus' name, amen." I then believe that I have received it.

After all, the Scripture says that we can come boldly to the throne of grace in time of need (Heb. 4:16). I don't know about you, but I have learned that my "time of need" is every day. I've realized that I can't be successful without Him. Yet with Him and His grace, we can do all things.

You can trust Him to help you raise your own happy kids and give them the foundation they need to fulfill their individual destinies.

High Calling

Motherhood is a very high calling in the kingdom of God! The world would have us believe otherwise. This is because the Enemy is terrified of godly mothers. We are way more powerful than we realize. Families are under attack because marriage is a picture of Christ and His church, and families are a picture of our heavenly Father and us, His children. Have you noticed that the Enemy has been heavily pushing for any other lifestyle other than traditional marriage? That is because only traditional marriage has the power to create life. Not only that, traditional marriage is holy before the Lord, and within the marriage covenant, the Enemy has no foothold to steal, kill, and destroy.

The Enemy is terrified of godly parents raising their children to know who they are in Christ and teaching them the authority they have over all the power of the Enemy.

As godly mothers, we need to stand firm, knowing

that what we are doing is vital for God, His kingdom, and for our husbands and children. Being steadfast and faithful with our God-given role will produce great eternal rewards.

Colossians 3:23 states:

And whatever you do, do it heartily, as to the Lord and not to men, knowing that from the Lord you will receive the reward of the inheritance; for you serve the Lord Christ.

Just know, dear mother, that in everything you do, you are doing it as unto the Lord Jesus. When you change another diaper for the hundredth time. When you cook a meal for your family. When you vacuum the floors. When you wash the dishes. When you serve your husband and your children. All of these things that you do, you are doing them unto the Lord Jesus.

Before I had my first child, I thought I would be disappointed if people stopped giving me gifts and instead gave them to my daughter. However, when my daughter was born and people gave her gifts, I felt as though they were giving them to me. If people showed love toward my daughter, it was as if they were showing love toward me. It was also true that if they were unkind or harsh toward my daughter, it was like they were doing the same to me! As a matter of fact, I had more patience with people who were harsh toward me than toward my daughter.

A Mother's Reward

All of our children were given to us by God. We are taking care of them for the Lord. Therefore, everything we do in service to our husband and children, we are doing as unto the Lord. And from the Lord we will receive a reward.

In Matthew 25:31-46, Jesus talked about how He will one day judge the nations. (Remember the judgment seat I was talking about earlier?) At that time, He will separate the believers from the unbelievers. He will place the believers (or sheep) at His right hand and the unbelievers (or goats) at His left. To the sheep on His right, Jesus will say things like, "I was hungry and you gave Me food. I was thirsty and you gave Me something to drink. I was naked and you clothed Me. I was sick and you visited Me." Then the righteous will ask Him questions like, "When did we see You hungry and feed You?" and "When did we see You thirsty and give You something to drink?" The Lord will then reply, *"Inasmuch as you did it to one of the least of these My brethren, you did it to Me"* (Matt. 25:40).

I strongly believe that mothers will be amongst the righteous at the judgment seat, asking all of these things. Yet how often do we see the children God gave us hungry and feed them? Naked and clothe them? Thirsty and give them something to drink? Basically every day! Every time and every way we serve our husband and children, we are doing it unto the Lord Jesus, and He has a generous reward waiting for us for our faithfulness and obedience. We serve and give of ourselves with no thought of a return. We do it in secret, where nobody sees. We do it in humility and faithfulness, only motivated by love.

Why would you ever think, dear mother, that you are not truly great in the eyes of the Lord? Why would you think for a second that your calling is not among the greatest in the kingdom of heaven? It truly is. Every day you are storing up for yourself treasures in heaven. Every day you are bearing fruit for eternity. Every day you are humbling yourself. There will surely come a day when you will see for yourself the impact you have made in eternity, how thankful your heavenly Father is, and how exalted you will forever be in heaven.

So, love on your husband, and love on your children. This is the high calling bestowed upon you from heaven.

---

[1] https://www.goodreads.com/quotes/757798-you-cannot-keep-birds-from-flying-over-your-head-but   (retrieved 12/10/2017)

[2]   http://www.christianitytoday.com/ct/2017/november-web-only/top-10-misquoted-lines-from-cs-lewis.html (retrieved 12/10/2017)

About the Author

Dana Bellamy married and started her family at a young age. Wed to a US Marine, she was taken away from everything familiar in her home country of Australia, and moved halfway across the world. Dana felt like Abraham in Genesis, taken away from everything familiar and placed in a new and different land. Dana didn't know how to be a good wife or mother, so the Lord took her by the hand and led her on the journey of learning who He is and what His Word really says. He also taught her how to be a godly wife and mother.

Today Dana is a graduate of Charis Bible College Colorado, with a minister's license as well as an associate's degree in biblical studies. She and her husband are in their fifteenth year of marriage and have six precious children. Dana's family is known for their happy marriage and for the joy and obedience of their children. Dana regularly encourages wives and mothers on their important God-given assignment and helps them raise their own children to love the Lord and fulfill their God-given destinies.

Made in the USA
Coppell, TX
10 December 2021

67788186R00095